Social Persuasion

Social Persuasion

Making Sense of Social Media for Small Business

ROBBIN BLOCK

Publisher's Cataloging-In-Publication Data
(Prepared by The Donohue Group, Inc.)

Block, Robbin.

   Social persuasion : making sense of social media for small business /Robbin Block. -- 1st ed.

   p. : ill., charts ; cm.

   Includes bibliographical references and index.
   ISBN: 978-0-9826013-0-3

1. Internet marketing. 2. Small business marketing--Data processing. 3. Social media--Economic aspects. 4. Online social networks--Economic aspects. I. Title.

HF5415.1265 .B45 2010
658.8/72   2010900795

Printed in the United States of America

DESIGN BY ROBBIN BLOCK
First Edition

For Mom, the first member of my social network.

And for all those who help me see the forest for the trees.

CONTENTS

Part V: Tracking Results

Part VI: Skills & Ingredients

Part VII: Where Do We Go from Here?

Acknowledgements

This book takes inspiration from the many people I've met who are willing to brave entrepreneurship, as well as from those writing about social media marketing as it takes shape.

I'd also like to thank all of my friends and family who have put up with me talking about "the book" for over a year now.

I'd especially like to thank Christi Williford, for her design guidance, Robert Lani and Adriana Medina for allowing me to use their images on the cover, and my editors, Bernard Bossom, Vicki Cohen and especially Brandon Smith who read the entire galley and provided detailed feedback, even while managing to ace many of his courses.

INTRODUCTION: The Digital Soft Sell

If you haven't heard by now, social technologies (a.k.a. social media, social networking) are hot, hot, hot. But there's nothing new about using the Web for communicating. Just like the browser made the Internet more accessible and fostered its growth, social media tools have made it easier to upload and share content. That's why people are flocking to it. This in turn is driving a whole new industry with a growing list of companies developing tools and services to make it faster and more fun.

What does this mean for businesses? Basically, that companies are no longer the only ones doing the communicating. Consumers are talking amongst themselves about the latest, greatest products, where to buy them and how they feel. They're creating their own content, and sharing it with their friends, family, colleagues and contacts. They're often bypassing and sometimes ignoring marketing messages as irrelevant or less trustworthy than what they're getting from their virtual networks. The tables are turning, giving customers a stronger position than they ever had before to influence the products that are bought and sold.

> Social media is more affordable than advertising, more accessible than public relations and more comprehensive than yellow pages.

Social media is also giving small businesses something that wasn't available before – a way to promote their products and services that's more affordable than advertising, more accessible than public relations and more comprehensive than yellow pages.

Social Persuasion is an oxymoron. Behind the scenes, businesses need to be strategic and practical when it comes to using social media to promote their wares. But social media is about conversations and engagement. The public persona needs to be unwitting and indirect, subtly coming across as the mentor, partner or friend. It's socially inappropriate and less effective from a marketing standpoint to blatantly advertise when posting to a blog or participating in a social network.

In many cases, social media can take longer to get results, since it depends on others to pass along information – to recommend, refer and share. If that information is fiery enough, word may spread quickly, but in most cases, it's a longer-term deal. Yet, it's more credible and effective when someone else besides you is doing the talking.

Social media is a two-way street. The duality of simultaneously being the visitor and the contributor makes it entirely co-dependent. You're watching people and people are watching you. This transparency can be a bit disconcerting and can get you into trouble, which means you need to be vigilant about what you do. What you say can come back to bite you – which in some cases may be just what you want.

Despite the fact that millions of people are using it, not all businesses are taking advantage of this new medium.[1] They're either unfamiliar with it, think it's a waste of time, perhaps believing that it's just for kids, or they're not sure where to begin.

This gap, between people using social media and the businesses who have yet to embrace it, presents business owners with an opportunity to break through all the marketing clutter to promote at a pretty affordable price – if they use it strategically. I say pretty affordable because even though most of the tools are free, the time it takes to make them work is the true cost of social media.

January 2010

About the Book

This book takes a strategic approach to using social media to benefit your business, answering the question, "What role should social media play in my marketing effort?" By the end, you'll know when to use it and how to figure out the right way to achieve your business objectives without letting it take over your life.

The main idea is to make the connection between established marketing practice and social media. Unlike other books and websites being written on the subject, the aim is to teach you how to fish, not to give you every tip, trick and magic way to get 5,000 followers on Twitter. It's about showing you how to make your own decisions about what makes sense for your business, how much attention you should pay to social media and how much of your resources you should invest, even as your business and the social space evolves.

For the most part, this book is about using social media to promote and grow your business in the most efficient way possible. It's not about building social network websites, how to earn money directly with social tools, like blogs, or using it for customer support – although many companies are putting it to good use in these areas.

Once you understand how social media works and what it can do for your business, you can make better choices about when and how to use it. (In this book, I explain what social media is and how it's used. There are so many websites and books on the topic, and social media is so dynamic, that it's almost impossible to talk about everything that's happening right now.) The idea is to teach you the fundamentals, so you can make better decisions about what to do and how to use the new tools, even as they evolve.

Part I goes into the basics of social media, who's using it, and the pros and cons of real and virtual networking. Part II explains the various types of social sites and what people typically do with them. Part III explains how to choose the right communication methods to incorporate into your marketing strategy. Part IV talks about implementing social media campaigns, and Part V shows you how to measure social media's value. Part VI gives you the skills to network successfully, including what to say and what to avoid. In the final section, we look to the future, which is to say the very near future, because it's changing as we speak.

The book also includes lists of action items to help you prioritize your social media activities with the aim of helping you overcome the inertia that comes with trying something new.

Who will benefit most from this book?

Small business owners, marketers and pretty much anyone else who wants to use social media in a strategic way to promote their businesses. It's for people who can see beyond the hype to realize that social media works best as an integrated part of a well-conceived marketing strategy.

It may also be useful for those who are planning to hire people to implement social media for them, whether that's an employee, freelancer or boutique agency. The book will help the reader understand social media from a broad perspective, while giving them an understanding of all the moving parts. Plus, it contains plenty of guidelines and checklists for managing the people and the process.

For marketers new to the techniques, the book can also serve as a checklist for planning and evaluating a communications program that incorporates social media.

Part I: The Social Media Scene

Definition & Purpose
Reality vs. Virtuality
The Business Benefits
The Participants

Chapter 1: Definition & Purpose

Before we get too far along, I want to clarify how I use some of the terms. The world of social media is so new that the terminology is a moving target. The terms *Social media* and *social networking* are often used interchangeably.

Social media generally refers to websites featuring user-generated content or material created by visitors rather than the website publishers. In turn, these sites encourage visitors to read and respond to that material.

There are two ways to think about how social media is used. One is when a website is entirely designed as a social entity, like the popular social networking site Facebook. The other is to think about social media as a utility. In other words, any website can incorporate social components to increase traffic, interactivity and visitor engagement.

Social media websites can be more than the familiar blogs and networks. They take other forms, like online event calendars (Yahoo's Upcoming), content sites (YouTube) and bookmarking (Digg). We'll talk about all the categories in Part II. I've chosen not to include auction and exchange sites, like eLance, Craigslist, Angie's List and the like, even though they allow for users to generate content. These are more like directories than what I think of as social sites, although the line could eventually blur with the addition of social features.

One need only a computer and an Internet connection to access a social site. Users can then add almost any type of information, like name, gender, age, the parties they attended, pictures, video, audio files...you name it. As long as it's digital, it can be added or uploaded. This information can then be made available to the user's network of family, friends, contacts and colleagues.

A Game Changer

Social media is changing the way people communicate and behave. One reason is that people want to express themselves creatively and show it off. Another is that users want to state their opinions and

Social media lives in the world of Web 2.0

Web 2.0 is often used to describe social media, but I define it more broadly as database driven websites offering personalization and interactivity. Web 1.0 may be defined as websites that are basically brochure-ware – ones with content, but without interactivity or an exchange of information between the site and the visitor. Web applications, like the Web-based customer relationship management tool Salesforce.com, is a good example of Web 2.0. Another well-known example is Amazon's ability to recommend book titles based on prior purchases.

hold conversations. This isn't new, but digital technology has made it so much easier to capture images, create video and make personal recordings. The format is entirely portable, which means it can be viewed on the desktop or on the go with a mobile device like a smartphone or iPhone.

Ego is a big part of it, too. Youth-oriented social networks like MySpace and Facebook saw rapid growth not only because they made it easier to create personal Web pages, they were essentially a popularity contest to see who could get the most friends.

Being able to express oneself is one thing but sharing it instantaneously is entirely another. Social sites make it easy to share information with friends, family, contacts, colleagues or people with similar interests. The upside is that social media is a vehicle for exploding this material all over the World Wide Web. On the other hand, it exposes the author to that same wide world. That's true whether you're an individual sharing a photo from a party or a business posting its mission to a blog.

Social sites have become more than a destination for socializing. "Many social network users repeatedly check their pages throughout the day to check messages and interact with friends. This frequent usage has caused social networks to evolve into a portal or starting point for many online sessions,"[2] depending on what the user is trying to do. When looking for a restaurant for example, rather than doing a general search or reading a newspaper review, they're looking to see where people are eating on a social review site like Yelp.

Personal referrals have always been important for making purchase decisions, but social media referrals are becoming an essential component of this process. Looking for advice, recommendations, referrals or any other type of information from one's social network is known as "social search." According to a DEI Worldwide 2008 report, "…consumers rely on various types of social media websites as much as company websites for product and brand information."[3] While the majority still begin their searches at search engines and portals, roughly 18% start with a social site.[4]

However, another study shows that even though one quarter of the people on a social network has recommended a business or product, only 18% have acted upon a recommendation. When they did, it was for entertainment (53%), dining out (50%), groceries (23%), beauty care/cosmetics (21%), apparel (20%), electronics (15%) and pet care (15%).[5] The fact that these categories rest on recommendations makes sense. Each can be rather difficult to distinguish and define, so people look to others for advice. However, for groceries, people seem to be bargain hunting, and most people are basing their recommendations on price and convenience.[6]

Companies used to be in control of the conversation – not so much anymore. In the olden days, businesses used advertising to promote their products, but they didn't expect people to talk back in a public way. If a person had problems with their purchase, only the company got the feedback – unless, of course, the media got wind of it. Now that seems an archaic notion, because voicing an opinion on the Internet is easy and instantaneous.

The trick for a business is to figure out how to get in on the conversation to reap the benefits without alienating anyone. That is, without coming across as a blowhard or sales pitchman, but as a trusted and valuable resource.

Social Media – What's Included?

Social media goes beyond blogs and social networks to include several key categories:

Blogs Allow for periodic communications in a diary format. Sometimes serve in place of websites. Example: BoingBoing

Microblogs Like a blog, but limited to 140 characters in length. Used for immediate communications, like announcements and alerts. Includes delivery via mobile phone. Example: Twitter

Social Networks Designed for building communities of people with mutual interests. Can incorporate other social media types, discussion boards, forums and email lists. Example: Facebook

Social Content Sites Primarily contain user-generated assets, like pictures, video, audio, slideshows, articles and more. May be referred to as "channels." Example: YouTube

Shopping & Review Sites Where visitors give opinions about products and services based on their own experiences. Review sites are especially useful for connecting service providers, restaurants and retailers with a local audience. Example: Yelp

Social Bookmarking Allows users to store, organize, search, manage and share websites, news and other information they come across on the Web. Example: StumbleUpon

Online Calendars Allow users to find and post events and link to other social sites to share calendars. Example: Yahoo's Upcoming

Wikis Self-policing websites or web pages where anyone with permission can add or modify content. Example: Wikipedia

Social Applications Tools that facilitate connections. Plaxo, for example, is an online address book that instantly updates when a user changes their profile. Example: Friendfeed

Email There are many tools available to help create and manage email communication, which is essential for extending and maintaining relationships beyond a social site. Example: MailChimp

Social sites are being created to appeal to all types of user groups and demographic clusters. The mainstream sites that millions of people are using include Facebook, LinkedIn and Twitter. Then there are niche sites catering to consumers, like Yelp, and those designed for business people, like Biznik. There are sites for travelers, like Trip Advisor, and those for people getting married, like The Knot. And those targeted at specific industries, like Myarchn for architects. What's important for your business is to figure out which ones will get you in front of the people with whom you want to communicate, which will be discussed in Chapter 14.

What People Do at Social Sites

People use social media for many reasons, including socializing (duh), publishing, marketing, research or work. For casual visitors, specific activities may include writing or commenting on a blog, inviting friends to their network, submitting articles, rating videos, voting, joining groups and more. It just depends on what is available at the site. I'll go into more detail about common activities on social sites later.

As a promoter, what you choose to do depends on what you're trying to accomplish. To figure that out, you'll need to determine the role social media should play in your company's marketing strategy. At the very least, your target audience needs to be using it. In other words, why worry about writing a post or uploading a video, if your potential customers aren't visiting the site where you're making a contribution? That's what Part III explains.

Is Social Media a Waste of Time?

Determining if social media is a waste of time depends on what you expect it to do for you. In that respect, social media is no different than other marketing tools. Use it well, use it strategically, and it won't be. And for the most part, it won't cost you anything out-of-pocket to participate. But don't be fooled. Just because you can use many social tools for free doesn't mean it's a no-cost way to communicate. It can take a lot of your valuable time, and if there's no return on that investment, then that's truly high cost.

Let's put it this way. You could spend hours and hours on social media tools, or you could put together a newsworthy press release that gets placed in a magazine with a circulation of 10,000. What's better? It all depends on what you're selling, the audience and all the other things we'll talk about later in the book.

Trying to get ranked high in search engines is a similar issue. You could spend a lot of time maintaining that top position, but if most of your clients come through referral, why would you bother? I'd spend more time on networking, public speaking and publishing articles, because people want to know you before they hire you. Getting ranked higher in search engines may get you website traffic, but not paying customers. Popularity is nice, but it doesn't pay the bills.

Is social media a fad?

Well, yes and no. Marketing hasn't changed much, at least in the past 80 years or so. But marketers being who they are, are always looking for new ways to position themselves against the competition to win more clients (and sell more books). They reshape the ideas into something that sounds more exciting than what came before, because revolution is a lot more marketable than evolution. But are the ideas really that new?

Branding took hold back in the early 20th century. *Relationship Marketing* came on the scene in the 1970's. And then of course, there have been big changes in media. Radio came along in the 1920's.

Commercial television followed about twenty years later. In the 90's, it was the Web (and everyone thought it would replace brick and mortar retail). Now social media is the latest thing. But even social interaction on the Web isn't new; it's just become easier to do, so more people are jumping in. But at the end of the day, as a business, you still need to nail down the basics – like your goals and target audience. That hasn't changed much. Once you figure those out, you'll be ready to decide if social media is the right medium for you.

Chapter 2: Reality vs. Virtuality

Social networking used to mean going somewhere to meet and mingle with other people. These days, it can take place at a live event or online. Meetup, a longstanding online network of local groups, is a good example of a site that gives people an easy way to organize live get-togethers.

For an appreciation of virtual networking, let's take a look at some of the pros and cons of real networking. First of all, it's 3-D, the full experience. All five senses are engaged – hearing the voice, with its tones and phrasing, seeing the mannerisms, making eye contact. We're firing our brains on all cylinders, so we're more involved, which makes it more meaningful and therefore memorable. Even if it's a first meeting, real networking feels more personal than "meeting" someone on the Web. In the digital space, something gets lost in translation. Consider attending a party versus watching one on television. 2-D just isn't the same.

There's nothing quite like face-to-face contact, but the combination can be more efficient – some of the time spent at live events can be replaced with online networking for example.

Networking virtually can also extend the value of participation in a live event. For example, often you don't know who people are until you talk to them. And as everyone knows, there are times you join in and you wish you had an out. Before you know it, you've wasted a whole hour with the wrong people. Going online before an event lets you check out the profiles of the people who have RSVP'd. Then,

When it comes to human relations, nothing replaces a real handshake and someone looking in your eyes.

By maintaining eye contact, you can tell when or whether people are paying attention to you, when people are involved in what you are saying, and whether what you are saying is eliciting feelings. Intensity of eye contact may be used to exercise dominance.[4] Eye contact also allows us to monitor the effect of our communication. If you're trying to persuade someone to do something, and you want to come across with as much credibility and confidence as possible, make eye contact when you're speaking.[5] Conversely, you may just be able to tell when someone is trying to *sell you* or pull the wool over your eyes.

What's available in the face-to-face situation that's lacking online?[5]

- Eye contact
- Facial expression
- Gesture
- Posture
- Movement
- Vocal characteristics: pitch, volume, rate, quality, phrasing
- Self-presentation: clothing, personal grooming, poise, touch, time

you can choose the people you want to meet and have a plan of approach before you go. Afterwards, you can go online to maintain connections with the people you met.

Social Spaces

Often, characteristics of a meeting place get associated with the people who manage and attend an event. And being seen with the right people can make a difference, too. This is known as the halo effect, and it applies to the social media space, as well. For example, there's a big difference between MySpace vs. LinkedIn. If you're in a band, MySpace, which attracts a young audience, could be just right. If you're a consultant, being seen on that site could be damaging to your credibility (on the slim chance your customers are hanging out there too). At the very least, you're going to seem out of place. Context is just as important as what you're trying to say. Put in Marshall McLuhan's terms, the medium is the message.[7]

How people and objects are arranged in a room can be significant, too. When you're at a live networking event, you can move around. You can see groups of people and the ones you want to meet. Surfing through photos on a website isn't quite the same as scanning a room for your next opportunity. Of course, a web cam would let you scan a room virtually, but social sites as we've defined them don't let you choose who you want to approach. Virtual worlds, like Second Life, are the only ones allowing this type of interaction at the moment. Not only that, they're creating connections with real world businesses.

Imagine being interviewed by someone behind a big desk in a huge office chair. Impressive? Intimidating? You betcha. Technology can be just as bad when it comes to a social site. Poor website design and confusing information can cause a visitor to avoid participation or leave the site altogether. That didn't necessarily stop users of MySpace, which has a fairly freeform look and feel. As a matter of fact, that could be why the site attracts so many music groups (beyond its appeal to a younger audience overall). But by the same token, that may be why Facebook has grown faster. It has a simpler and more uniform interface.

The point is that the design of a social space has an impact on who will use it and how they participate. And, the way you engage with a site will have an impact on how people respond to your material. The information you provide about your business has to be just as clear, just as easy to find, and set the right tone to be effective. We'll discuss this further in Part VI.

Another benefit to virtuality is that you can meet whole communities of people. At a live event, you just won't have the time to meet everyone. Online, you can join groups to meet and converse with lots of people at once, and meet people outside of your own network. They can be from outside your local area, too.

Social Skills Required

The beauty of going to a live event, as I've described, is that it's more engaging. That is of course, if you're an engaging person. You need social skills to make that work. You've got to look and act the part, pick out the right people to meet, not be afraid to speak with total strangers, be somewhat articulate, be able to tell your story, gauge the response (are you boring them? are they interested? are they zoning out? are they interested in what you offer?), etc. Not everyone feels comfortable with this, no matter how much practice they get. It's a personality thing.

Virtuality can be a star for people with less than stellar social skills. You can be as anonymous or eponymous as you desire. You can lurk behind a pseudonym, although this is not recommended for business – it can seem devious. If you don't want to use your name, and you represent a business, group or association, you can use that name.

Writing Skills Required

Face-to-face networking is spontaneous. You have to look good and be able to think on your feet, unless of course, you have an agenda or notes, but you can't very well stand there with a list in your hands. With social media, you can prepare.

The challenge, though, is that you have to do the work. That is, write, upload, and create content to participate in a valuable way. Playing games, as you might with friends on Facebook, won't get you the exposure you're after.

There's a lot of time, energy and hard work involved, but you can control your own story. You can write something and edit it before uploading. In a live situation, you can slip pretty easily. No edit or undo buttons. Plus, written communication often carries more weight than the spoken word; it may be taken more seriously. Something said at a live event can easily evaporate. If it's important enough and you want it to last, post it online.

Material provided online may be a stronger way to spread the word, because the viral nature of the Web allows you to extend your reach through hyperlinks. This can be good and bad. Say something once, and it gets picked up by other sites or shared by other users. People can print, paraphrase and save it through links, sharing tools, applications and search bots (a computer program that searches the Web automatically). That's a strength of going virtual that can't be replicated in the real world, and that's the multiplier effect that gives social media (and all online media) its power. The downside is just that – once you put it out there and it gets shared, you can't take it back.

Chapter 3: Business Benefits

Let's face it, all this participation in social media may be free, but it takes a lot of time and energy to do it right. And as they say, time is money, especially for a small business. So you need to decide if it's the most efficient and effective use of your valuable resources. You also need to figure out how much to allocate to social media as opposed to other marketing activities.

The first step in resolving these issues is to determine what you're trying to accomplish. Let's start by taking a look at what you can expect to get out of social media.

Market Research: Lurk, Crowdsource & View Site Data

Whether you're writing a business plan, need customer feedback or want to learn more about your competition or industry, social sites can be a great source for market research. There's a wealth of information if you know what you're looking for and where to look. Lurking, crowdsourcing and digging into a social site's data are just some of the ways to find it.

Just realize that using social media for research can be anecdotal at best. Without a significant number of responses, you need to be careful about thinking that this limited amount of data reflects how everyone would respond. This is especially true for comments or reviews.

Be aware of the built-in bias – answers are coming from a specific group of people who are active social site participants. That means you may not get a complete picture of everyone in your target audience. Credibility is a factor, too. People can pretty much say what they want, and there's no guarantee the information is coming from a qualified source. Check the writer's credentials and their motives, the site where the information appeared and the publication date. It's a good idea to second source the material, as well.

Go Undercover

Lurking occurs when someone visits and accesses a site's information without joining or participating. It's a way to go undercover to see what people are saying, learn about competitors, check backgrounds of potential employees, etc. Simply reading through comments on a blog post can provide more information than the post itself. Review sites can be especially useful for customer feedback. Just look for mentions of your company name or product. If you aren't listed, then that tells you something, too. Either you need to get listed, or no one is providing feedback.

Clouds Tell a Story

Another information source is the tag or word cloud, which appears on many social sites. Words representing the topics are shown in various sizes and colors according to their popularity. It can give you a sense of what's being talked about on a site.

Word Cloud active client inquiry interior designer intern it job hunter linkedin logos mailing lists marketing folk media mobile mybook mybook editor mypublicity photographer potential client pr printer radio radio guest real estate recruiter research school score client score counselor signage signs slu social media speaker speakers bureau **speaking** squarespace designer startups **student** team television templates trade vendor venue video videography web design wireless wordpress writer

Strength in Numbers

Crowdsourcing is a technique for getting the collective power of the Web to do a job for you. You can use social media for polling your audience to answer questions like, "What should I name my product?" The question and answer (Q&A) area of a social site may be used for this purpose. Before posting your own question, you might want to search the Q&A of a site to see what people want to know, the services they're looking for or to learn about a particular industry or business problem.

Microblogs can be used for posting questions too, like, "What's the best online business card printer?" You can use a tool like Twtpoll to create surveys for Twitter. Getting people to respond to surveys is the hard part though. Many questions go unanswered or only a few people bother, which could make it a pointless exercise.

Site-Specific Tools

Many sites offer a way to gather information about the people using it. For example, in LinkedIn's footer you'll find a tool for creating polls. You can also use their advanced search to find leads, company information, and people with similar interests by city. Sometimes you can tell when people are changing jobs or looking for employment – the tip off is when they update their profiles.

Facebook offers Lexicon, which counts how often certain terms appear across profiles, groups and event walls each day – the information is aggregated, which means it's not tied to any specific profile. You can then customize your search and view results in multiple ways, such as by number or percentage of posts, gender, age, and geography.

Media Kits

Many sites are seeking advertisers, so they're willing to share information about their users in what is generally called a *media kit*. Look for it via the advertising links in the footer of the site. If you can't find one, you might try contacting their advertising sales department, but you may have to field questions about your marketing plans. Simply say you're in the budgeting stage and not ready to buy, but be prepared for the follow up calls and emails.

More Ways to Count

Third-party services, like Alexa, Compete and Quantcast offer data about social sites, too. They'll let you know how popular a web site is, its rank, and how fast it's growing. Bizshark compares the activity of competitors. We'll talk more about this in Chapter 14.

Awareness, Name Recognition & Top-of-Mind Awareness

The first step in any marketing strategy or communication plan is to make people aware of a business's existence. The next step is to achieve "name recognition" – getting them to remember the name. And getting them to recall the product or service just when they're ready to buy is what is known as "top-of-mind awareness." Joining networks, listing a company on review sites and promoting a blog are just some of the ways a business can use social media to achieve these objectives. We'll go much deeper on this topic in Part III.

Brand Building, Reputation & Word-of-Mouth

When I talk about branding here, I'm not referring to what is called visual identity, comprised of a company's logo, colors, fonts, audio tags, etc. A brand, in the marketing sense, is the result of experiences and communications that make up a consumer's thoughts and feelings about a company, product or entity. Brands are especially useful when consumers are making decisions about purchasing confusing, complex or status items – otherwise known as "high involvement" products or services.

Unlike creating awareness that a product or service exists, building brand is about letting people know what the business stands for – it needs to be authentic and believable, that is, upheld by the core concept, business model and consistent messaging.

Social media can be great for personal branding, but it hasn't proven as effective, at least not yet anyway, for company branding. Advertising is often the communication method used to build a brand, but it's been shown that social media participants often ignore ads. According to a study from WorkPlace Media of employed consumers, the majority of respondents said their opinion of a brand doesn't change if it has no presence on a social networking site. Only 12% said it would.[8]

The *brand promise* is what a company implies or says it's going to deliver. It means setting customer expectations, and then consistently delivering on them over time. Reliable delivery and repetition builds trust, remembrance and reputation. In a social setting, sharing useful information and expertise is one way to build a positive reputation and amplify word of mouth.

"After searching, online consumers said they are most likely to communicate with others about their search through face-to-face discussion (68.9%), although email (53.1%), telephone (50.9%), and cell phone (30%) communication were also popular choices," RAMA [Retail Advertising and Marketing Association] says. Young adults (18-24) also say they send IM's [Instant Messages] about what they've learned (37.5%), text message (23.7%), and use outlets like online communities like MySpace and Facebook (20.6%)."

If you're a plumber, for example, you may tell customers that you're always available in an emergency. Answering the office phone on the third ring may be a way to reinforce that brand promise. A way to visually communicate the brand to customers might include an illustration of a plumber driving a fast-moving ambulance. Offering tips for plumbing emergencies on a social site may be used to create a positive reputation.

Networking, Partnerships & Relationship Building

It's almost redundant to say that social networking sites help you find people for partnering, sharing ideas, referrals and more. Once those relationships are created, it provides an ideal way to create interaction to keep it going. We'll talk more about how to do this in Chapter 15.

Website Traffic, Search Rankings & Stickiness

For the small business, once someone is aware of a business, especially if found online, they're likely to visit the website. That makes building awareness one of the key reasons to participate in social media. When you post, whether that's at a social networking site, on someone else's blog or upload a new image or thought, there's a chance that someone will want to know more and go to your site.

Search engines, like Google, use words to find and organize information. They send out spiders (small, automated computer programs) to find and count the number, location and context of those words on all types of sites, including social ones. However, not all social sites are visible to search engines. For example, a person's Facebook profile will only be visible to Google if their privacy settings are set to public.

People seeking information type words into search tools. The result is a search engine results page or SERP. Where a site appears on the SERP depends on the formula or *algorithm* used by the search engine to rank the results. Inbound links from other sites are also an important part of that formula, based on the idea that a site will be more relevant to the searcher if many other sites find it useful, too.

Therefore, the words you choose to include in your site, or when participating socially, should be the ones your potential customers are using to find products or services like yours. Known as *keywords*, they're the digital DNA of any online marketing program. If you want your site, social site submissions, press releases and anything else you put online to count, you need to include them. When you're mentioned on social sites, you'll have a better chance of being found. Increasing that incidence of mentions and links is a key benefit of participating in social media.

Stickiness happens when a website visitor views several pages, stays for a longer period or returns to your site repeatedly. Because they're spending more time at your site, there's a good chance they're going to get to know you and what you have to offer. This gives you a chance to build a relationship with them. They'll begin to remember you, and when they have a need for your type of product or service and are ready to buy, they'll contact you. This increase in engagement is one way to measure the value of social media.

Leads, Referrals & Sales

Creating awareness is one way to generate sales leads for a business. Another is to get referrals. That means building up a network of people who serve the same audience as you do, but who aren't competitors. Then, you can communicate with them on a regular basis, so they remember you when they hear of someone needing a product or service you offer. One way to maintain that connection is to send them referrals, anticipating that they'll return the favor.

Social media not only helps build connections between related businesses, it offers some specific ways to generate leads, too. LinkedIn, for example, combines their data with company profiles, which can be researched to develop targeted leads lists.

Keywords and Tags

Keywords are made up of one word, or a two to three word phrase that people use for plugging into search engines to find information. The importance of keywords should not be underestimated.

When it's not possible to naturally include keywords in the body of what is being written, they often can be added as tags. Tags are also useful when non-text content, like videos and images, need to be identified, because search engines can't "see"; they can only search for words.

Here are some ways to come up with your own keyword list:

- Imagine what people might use to search, such as familiar industry terms, your company name, your name, etc.
- Try using keywords at least 2 words long.
- Check out the keyword tool offered by Google Adwords, which shows keyword popularity and offers suggestions.

Social media can help you make a sale, too. For example, someone called me recently and name-dropped someone I knew – presumably they found it on LinkedIn. That helped to break the ice and warm up the call. He was also able to learn a thing or two about me from my LinkedIn page. That is, he was able to find a connection or something in common with me to help him build trust on the call. On the other hand, as soon as I got off the phone, I checked him out on LinkedIn and followed up with the friend we had in common to check the legitimacy of his claims. Let's just say I'm glad I did.

Outreach, Customer Service, Retention & Loyalty

Social media provides a way for companies to maintain relationships and foster loyalty by helping them keep in touch with customers on a regular basis. According to a 2008 Cone Business in Social Media Study, "56% say they feel a stronger connection with and better served by companies when they can interact with them in a social media environment."[10] Giving customers the ability to communicate directly with a company helps build loyalty. Zappos, the successful online shoe store, is well known for their online customer support they provide via Twitter. These positive experiences can also turn customers into company advocates.

Giving customers the feeling that they're part of an exclusive group or part of a community is another way to foster loyalty. It makes them feel special. Social networking sites, particularly ones that carve out a niche, are especially good at this because people want to connect with like-minded individuals. They can "relate" to each other and are more trusting of each other's opinions.

Chapter 4: The Participants

Social media offers the small business many benefits, but you still need to determine if it's right for your situation. If your audience isn't using it, then it's not going to work for you. Netpop Research says social networking grew 93% between 2006-2008.[11] In the same period, Facebook grew 500%.[12] Despite the tremendous growth, you need to understand how that breaks down in terms of who uses it, how much, why and what they do at the sites, to determine the extent of your investment in it. Let's take a look at who's using social media today.

The social media landscape continues to grow and evolve. Since only an Internet connection is needed to access a social site, its use is beginning to parallel the typical Internet user. And that's pretty much everybody, including the 1.5 billion people in the world who have Internet access, more than 300 million with broadband access to the home, and the 3 billion with cell phones.[13] As the popularity of social media continues to rise, it's getting harder to identify a typical social media user.

Social media users need to be Web savvy, at least to a degree. If they're not, it's unlikely they're going to be on social networks, let alone active users of them. The book Groundswell talks about how older users are more likely to simply read content; not create and upload material.[14]

Users should be able to access the Internet and be familiar with a browser, such as Internet Explorer, Firefox, Safari or Chrome. It's helpful if they have some basic skills, like navigating a site and uploading content, like articles and images. More advanced users know some HTML, understand widgets and applications, and know what it means to embed code. This allows them to really take advantage of all that social sites have to offer. The same is true for you – the more advanced your ability to use social sites, the more you can leverage them to your benefit.

Users also need to feel secure – some people are afraid to submit personal information, and this may limit their participation or keep them from using social media altogether. Other barriers to social media adoption may include language, culture, and restrictions based on company policy or legal issues.

Social User Segmentation

As we've seen, all types of people use social media and for different purposes. Consumers use them for vanity reasons or to boost their egos by being first or popular. They make themselves stand out by personalizing their presence and voicing their opinions by voting for favorite bands or TV shows. In fact, entertainment industry websites "are among the top beneficiaries of upstream traffic from [niche social networking sites] outside of search, email and other social networking websites. Education and sports follow… ."[15] They may have the desire to meet people, socialize and build relationships. The rationale could be practical, like finding long-lost friends or a great restaurant.

Contrary to what you may think, that social media sites are for youngsters, 35% of adult Internet users have a profile on a social network, more than quadrupling in the last four years.[16] But, you're partly right. It skews young, with 75% of 18-24 year olds using them compared to just 7% of adults 65 and older.

Business users are looking for employees, partnerships, new business, and for all the other reasons discussed in the last chapter. But remember, business users are people, too. A 2009 study by Workplace Media shows that working people are dividing their time between professional and personal networking. 89% of respondents reported having a Facebook account, 40% were on MySpace; 31% were on LinkedIn and 18% Twitter. 89% said the main reason they participated was that it let them stay connected to friends/family.[17]

Segmentation is one way to make sense of the vast number of users and the types of sites they prefer to visit. They are clustered along shared characteristics, like geography, demographics, psychographics and behaviors (see Chapter 9). You may be familiar with some well-known consumer market segments like Yuppy (Young Urban Professional), Generation X and Y, and Soccer Mom.

Many social sites define themselves along these lines, as well. For example, BOOMj, TeeBeeDee, Classmates Online and Eons are designed to appeal to another familiar segment, Baby Boomers. Placing your potential customers into certain social segments will make it easier for you to figure out how to find the best ways to research, reach and effectively communicate with your target audience. Let's take a look at some examples of segmentation as applied to social media.

Age can be a strong indicator (but not the only one as we'll see) of how social media is being used. Patricia Brusha begins by defining *Social Butterflies*, aged 15-25. These individuals flit to different sites based on popularity among their peers. They use social sites for sharing photos, videos and blog post with their networks. As a marketer, you need to get involved in their community to "capture their attention." One way to do that is by creating groups targeted at their interests. "Butterflies are more likely to go directly to communities bypassing search to find what they are looking for. If they like what they see, they will be sure to tell their friends and family." [18]

This group, having grown up with the Web, is very comfortable using social media. They also seem to have a lot more time to play with it than older adults, aged 25-45, who have other things on their minds, like an established group of friends, children and jobs with greater responsibility. Brusha defines these adults as *Socially Selective*. Most people in this age range have been using the Web for years and are very comfortable with social media as well, but are accustomed to more traditional ways of communicating. They're more likely to use social sites to get something done, like planning a wedding or a trip, because their time is more limited than the butterflies.

Some of that time could be shifting, however, since there are some things that are easier to do through social media than by phone or even email, like sending photos and video – this group enjoys video and shorter blog entries. Traditionally big users of email, they're spending more time communicating through social networks. Their mainstream sites are Facebook, and they're using Twitter, Blackberry messenger or iPhone applications.[19]

"Having a clear purpose and staying niche focused is the way to successfully market to this demographic. People in this category are there for a reason; unlike social butterflies, they're on the site to accomplish something, not to be social first. Selectives want to feel they are part of an elite community, sharing only with others like themselves with similar passions."[20]

46-55 year olds use the Web about 90% of the time, and rarely use text messaging. Their use of microblogs is very low; they don't generally trust social media and they're skeptical of their content. They prefer to read hard copies than something on a computer screen. You're not going to reach this group through Twitter, but as mobile Internet usage increases, this group will probably get on board just like everyone else.[21] Brusha defines these as *Social Starters* who are beginning to become familiar with the term social media. When they realize there's more to it than Facebook and MySpace, which they believe is for kids, they're likely to try it. They're intrigued but not quite sure how to get started.[22]

Starters tend to find social media sites by accident or hear about them from a friend. They're more likely to request that a friend or one of their children find some time to explain it to them. It's not often clear what they should do or what the benefits are, and they're often skittish about providing personal information.

Some 56-65 year olds are using social media regularly to keep in touch with family, but their mobile consumption is relatively low. As the wireless market ages and remains more active than previous generations, this will change. So I imagine their use of social media while mobile will increase, as well.

As for the 65-year old plus group, many aren't comfortable with computers, they aren't really participating in social sites and their mobile consumption is mostly for voice. So there probably won't be much change for them in the near future.[23]

A new generation of consumers, or what Brusha calls the New Social Norms, which includes children, tweens and teens, are growing up in a Web 2.0 world. In their minds, social media sites are an accepted and familiar way of navigating the Internet, and there are plenty of sites to accommodate them. Sites like Club Penguin, Webkinz, Disney, Nickelodeon and Barbie are training children to expect interactive websites as the norm. To get them excited about a product, marketers need to come up with promotions that include features like secret codes, earning cash or points, daily and weekly contests, numerous activities, games and videos. However, you can't market to kids without paying attention to the parents. Terri Walter, VP of emerging media at Razorfish says, "...Almost half of the social-network users monitor their children's behavior online; and 40% of blog readers mind their children's blogging habits."[24]

He went on to say that, "...moms use [digital media] for themselves primarily and secondarily for their kids."

CafeMom segments the digital Mom audience into five segments, which provide clues into the behaviors: self-expresser, utility Mom, groupster, infoseeker and hyperconnector (the smallest segment, but the most digital). She's in her 40's and pretty much done with searching for parenting advice. She's more interested in finding online friends, blogging, personal messaging, and is most likely to answer questions and offer comments.

"They're most interested in fashion and food, regardless of age and their use of online video, blogs and DVRs have become mainstream, in the 29% to 36% range, while podcasting, RSS feeds and mobile-web browsing remain niche channels, used by 10% to 21% of respondents."

"They learn about new products from TV, friends and magazines, followed by e-mail, websites, podcasts, search engines and mobile-web browsing. Among mobile-internet users, web browsing was almost as important a new-product source as search engines in brokerage, telecommunications, electronics and cars."[25]

Social Media Behavior

Understanding what social media users do online will help you figure out what you should be doing to connect with them. As we've seen, age isn't the only indicator of usage. Behavior varies widely in terms of online comfort level, available time, purpose and many other factors. For example, most senior citizens have no idea what social media is, but they may visit social sites for particular reasons. My uncle is an avid traveler and loves planning trips – there's a good chance he uses Trip Advisor, but doesn't think of it as social networking.

Social media is having an impact on the way people use the Web in general. For example, more searches are taking place on YouTube than on the search portal Yahoo (ranked number two behind Google for search).[26] According to DEI Worldwide/OTX, consumers are using social media sites slightly more than they would company websites when searching for information.[27] This is another reason why it makes sense for businesses to have some kind of social presence in addition to a website.

Forrester Research has developed classifications for the types of things people are doing on social sites.[28] They include:

Creators   Publish Web pages, write blogs, upload videos, etc.

Critics   Comment on blogs; post ratings and reviews.

Collectors   Use RSS and tag Web pages to gather information.

Joiners   Use social networking sites.

Spectators   Read blogs, watch peer-generated videos, and listen to podcasts.

Inactives   Are online, but don't yet participate in any form of social media.

These classifications are then mapped to demographics in Forrester's online profiling tool, so you can make some predictions about your audience's behaviors. Understanding what they like to do online will help you decide if you should even be using social media to communicate with your audience, the types of sites that make sense and the content or interactive tools you should provide.

Business Users

At the moment, personal use seems more prevalent than professional use. This is probably because business users want to get something from their investment of time and energy. The ones that are involved are using it to connect with people they already know. Patricia Bruscha labels this group the *Socially Connected*.[29] They use social sites for business and career whether that's for finding leads, referrals, partners or jobs. The more useful the sites are in terms of the user's business goals, the more they'll be active on them.

"B2B buying is fertile ground for emerging community sites, social networks, and user-contributed content," said Laura Ramos, vice president and principal analyst at Forrester. "But most B2B marketers miss the nuances of their audience's preferences by jumping directly to deploying social technology without first profiling the social behavior of their customers. Knowing buyers' behavior lets marketers set the most effective social media strategy instead of blindly trying every new technology that comes along."[30] As an example, just because Facebook is the most popular social networking site, doesn't mean the industrial buyer in your target audience is using it for business.

According to the Forrester survey, technology decision-makers actively participate in social media as it relates to their jobs. Of the six categories in Forrester's Social Technographics Profile,[31] about 1/4 don't engage in social media activities for work purposes at all. Almost 70% are Spectators: they read blogs, listen to podcasts, watch video or read online forums and reviews. Of the remaining four categories, roughly 1/3 are Creators, Critics, Collectors and Joiners.

"Despite these activities, social media has yet to effectively influence a large part of the technology buying process. Fifty-one percent of survey respondents feel social media doesn't play an important role in the purchasing process, and 60 percent of survey respondents don't find blogs more valuable than editorial content for informing purchase decisions. More than three-fourths of respondents said peers influence their purchase decisions more than any other media or information source."[32] Business executives still turn to industry trade publications and the Internet for information.

Some are starting to use social media to tap into information from colleagues, and that will probably increase as social media evolves. A survey of CEOs, Senior Executives and Business Owners revealed:[33]

85% use business-networking sites to find new business opportunities.

90% rate exclusivity as a "very important" attribute of a business network.

93% want real-time interaction within a business network.

All this depends on how technology-focused a user is. Market research firm New Diligence surveyed 527 end users and IT managers and found about 60% of respondents use social networks at work, while 85% use IM [instant messaging] and media, including streaming audio and video.[34]

Just like consumer demographics, businesses can be segmented along certain characteristics, like industry and size measured by number of employees, revenue or seats. This is sometimes called *bizographics*. There are many business-related websites designed to match. LinkedIn, for example, is most popular with managerial professionals, especially when it comes to looking for jobs. Spoke and Naymz target a similar audience. Xing is for global connections. Biznik is designed for solopreneurs.

As I mentioned, social media may not be a good match for your target audience. A simple way to figure out if they're using it is to simply ask your current customers and business contacts. Keep checking back with them, because behaviors are changing rapidly. As the tools get simpler and people recognize the benefits of organizing their social lives online, more people will be jumping on board. We'll also begin to see more ways to classify and understand users. And more research will be done to explain what's happening and to justify spending in the space. And that will make us better at using social media for marketing.

Part II: The Playing Field

The Social Media Mix:

Blogs & Microblogs
Social Networks
Social Content Sites
Shopping & Review Sites
Social Bookmarking
Social Calendars
Wikis
Social Applications
Email

Properties: Your Digital Real Estate

Common Social Activities

Chapter 5: The Social Media Mix

Social media is comprised of many types of websites and tools. We'll briefly introduce them here and take a deeper look into how to use them for promotions later in the book.

Blogs & Microblogs

Blogs were one of the first types of social sites to really take hold. They started off as a way to post periodic entries, like an online diary of sorts, and gave authors a way to publish to the Web instantly. The blog form has evolved way beyond the personal diary, in some cases into full-featured, online magazines like Technorati and CafeMom.

Blogs may be standalone or added to an existing website. Blogger, which was created by Evan Williams, was one of the first tools that allowed users to build their own blogs easily. It was later purchased by Google. There are many others, including Typepad. WordPress, is fast becoming the tool of choice for building blogs that act as fully realized websites, thanks to its customizable features and built-in social widgets. In fact, my website and many of my clients' are hosted on a blog/content management system called Squarespace.

Adding a blog to an existing website is a great way for someone with more writing than technical skill to keep a site fresh. Blogs can also be a great place to include images and video (vlogs are blogs that are mostly videos). Contractors and landscapers can post pictures about their latest projects; consultants can talk about new ideas; financial professionals can offer seasonal tax tips.

Having a blog is one thing, but getting it noticed is quite another. It's not easy breaking through the 133 million blog glut that existed as of the end of 2008.[35] If you're going to use a blog effectively, it's going to have to be very interesting, highly targeted, and well promoted.

Although there was tremendous growth in the number of blogs, the growth rate has slowed. However, there has been a 300% rise in monthly blog readership over the past four years.[36]

Microblogs

The difference between blogs and microblogs is basically the length of the message. That's because microblogs are designed to work with mobile text messaging, which is limited to a certain number of characters (Twitter allows 140).[37] Microblogs, and in particular Twitter, have really grown in popularity because they're perfect for those who don't want to write as much as a blog or people with short attention spans (which seems like most of us these days).

At a microblog, a user can create an account for either public or private viewing. Once that's done, the user invites people to "follow" their posts (in Twitter lingo, that's a "Tweet"). Getting "followed" is a key aim of microblog users, because the bigger the number, supposedly the more people are reading their messages. Many people follow whoever follows them in knee-jerk fashion, and that has enabled many to acquire huge numbers of followers. However, users following so many people can't possibly read all the messages they get. For example, if I'm following 200 people on Twitter (and many people have thousands), and they're putting up two posts per day (and some do many more), that means I'd have to read 400 posts per day. That's not possible. So unless I'm actually doing a search by user or keyword, whether that's on Twitter or I've set up a tool to do the searches for me, there's a good chance I'm not going to actually see most of the messages.

That makes me question the value of a microblog for general promotion, but companies are using them in some interesting ways. Practical applications include customer support, project management and event reminders. In fact, there's a service called Yammer that makes it easy for a company to create their own microblog to help people within an organization stay connected. In addition, because the information is immediately available via mobile, microblogs are useful for posting updates and alerts. Imagine you're a real estate agent. You could tell your clients to follow you on Twitter, so they're kept informed about new listings on their mobile phones.

Social Networks

Often used interchangeably with the term social media, social networks are specifically designed to help create community among friends, families, colleagues, contacts and people with similar interests or cultural affiliation (otherwise known as affinity groups).

For consumers, there are mainstream sites like Facebook and MySpace, and niche sites like BoomJ for Baby Boomers. For managerial professionals, there's LinkedIn, and for solopreneurs, there's Biznik. There are many to choose from and more being added every day. If you're looking for a particular type of social networking site, Compete regularly publishes top-ranking lists. We'll talk more about how to find the right sites in Chapter 14.

Often, social networks are standalone websites. There are also tools that allow you to create your very own social network, like Ning, and others, like Google's Friend Connect, that provide you with widgets or plugins that allow you to incorporate social network-type functions into your website.

Link to	Integrate with	Promote thru
Create your own social network Ex: *Ning*	Add social widgets to your site Ex: *Google Friend Connect*	Leverage social site traffic Ex: *BakeSpace*

Becoming a member of a social network starts with signing up and creating a profile. Then the user is free to add content, pictures, links, events, etc., and to interact with the site and other members. Here are some of the more common features of social networks:

Profile pages: where members add, edit and enhance information about themselves.

Social bar: designed to give visitors easy access to social features.

Courtesy: Google Friend Connect

Member tool: shows the members of a network, typically in block format.

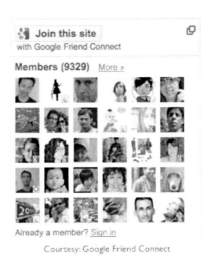

Courtesy: Google Friend Connect

Wall (AKA Activity Wall or User Stream): where comments from network members appear as they take place.

Review tools: where visitors can rate or review books, movies, videos, articles, photos, etc.

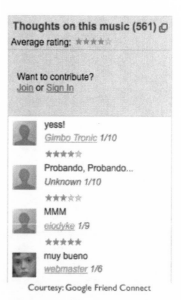

A Social Network of Your Very Own

There's a big difference between owning your own social space and simply being a participant. Maintaining your own social network takes a lot of time and energy, even if all the content is user-generated. You'll need to monitor the development, creation, and appropriateness of the content, while marketing it to drive traffic, membership and retention. Rather than create your own, it just might make sense to participate in an established site with a strong user base to leverage the effort someone else has made to build, maintain and market it.

Some good reasons for your own include having an existing membership base or source of members, a need for group communication, and the desire to create and market something of your own. If your intent is to make a social network into a business, rather than to enhance your website or as a marketing tool, that's another story for a different book.

Social Content Sites

All websites have content – the words, images and other things a visitor sees on a Web page. What makes social sites different is that people can interact with the site by adding content of their own, voting, posting, sharing, commenting, etc. If people aren't interacting, it's not really social – it's just content.

Some of the most well-known, mainstream social content sites include YouTube for videos, Flickr for photos, PodcastAlley for Podcasts, and SlideShare for slideshows. If you do anything original, this is where you need to be, whether you're an instructor, want to show an expertise in doing something, need to promote events, or whatever, you need to find a way to utilize these services to show off what you do. If what you post is popular, people will share it, too.

Shopping & Review Sites

Social shopping sites serve as a type of filter on the Web to help people determine what products to buy and where. They combine reviews, ratings and comparisons and allow visitors to post their comments and opinions. People can talk about finds, deals and recommendations. For the most part, shopping sites are distinguished from pure review sites by the fact that visitors can make purchases right there. They're a blog, magazine, review site and an online store rolled into one. Amazon has been at it the longest, with their extensive user-generated reviews of books and everything else they sell.

Review sites typically don't include ecommerce, especially if they offer intangible services. Some of these sites are more general in nature, offering reviews on all types of local businesses, from retail clothing to healthcare providers. Users write their own reviews or can vote for the ones they like, ask people to become friends, send messages and more. Others, like the travel site TripAdvisor, are more specialized.

Shopping and review sites are viewed to have more credibility and authenticity than anything a business can put on their own site. However, despite their growing influence, studies are showing that "real-life referrals are more influential to consumers than those received online."[38] "It's interesting to find that as much time as we spend online, we still prefer a personal recommendation from someone we know and trust," says Chris Haack, senior analyst at Mintel. "Young adults are somewhat more likely to turn to the Internet for advice and referrals, but even they listen to their peers first." [39]

What motivates people to write reviews?

"…Daphne Durham, books editor at Amazon, says some reviewers really do want to shape others' opinions. 'Someone out there is reading Harry Potter for the first time,' she says. This prompts other readers who feel strongly about it 'to debunk the hype, or to validate it.' On Amazon, indeed, the most prolific reviewers are promoted almost as celebrities in their own right. This prompts reviewers to focus on quantity, not quality, however, so Amazon recently changed its ranking system. Now the 'helpfulness' of reviews is taken into account, causing Harriet Klausner, the most prolific reviewer with over 18,000 reviews to her credit, to drop below 500th place in the rankings."[40]

Social Bookmarking

Sites like StumbleUpon, Delicious and Digg, let people save and share their favorite news stories, websites and more. They also allow people to store, organize, search, and manage their webpage bookmarks, and then share them with others. Bookmarks may be saved for public or private viewing, or shared with selected people or groups. Information can be organized with tags, categories and/or folders. They also incorporate many of the features of social networking.

One of the benefits of social bookmarking is that it serves as a filter for readers, narrowing the field down by tag or category. As social bookmarking becomes more popular, it's possible that people will go to tagged lists, rather than searching directly on a search engine, where the results may be too broad. Social bookmarks get the human touch (rather than a computer applying a mathematical formula to organize the data), which could make the information they provide more relevant (or not, if they're not tagged correctly).

Social Calendars

Social calendars aren't typically included in talks about social media, but they should be because small businesses often host, participate in or speak at events as a way to promote their businesses. They can be a good way to reach a local audience, because live events typically draw on a limited geographic area. Not all online calendars are social, however – I'm only referring to the ones that incorporate social components. Key advantages include the ability to share an event and to view profiles of those who have registered.

Online calendars, such as Upcoming and Eventful, allow you to search for events to attend, find others who are or who have attended events you're interested in, or post an event of your own. Some of these sites link together, which allows you to post in one place and have it also appear in another. For example, you can link your Upcoming events to your Facebook or LinkedIn accounts.

There are other tools that make it easy to share your calendar with your network and include them in your website. Google Calendar has probably been around the longest, but there are others like MatchboxCalendar, which helps you keep your network up to date with your schedule or events. Eventful has a widget that counts down the days until an event.

Wikis

Wikis are websites or web pages that allow anyone with permission to do so to make contributions or to modify content. One of the best known is Wikipedia, an online Wiki-based encyclopedia, which was started in 2001. Its founder also started Wikia. Other wikis include WikiHow, a how-to manual, and WikiMapia, a site that combines Google Maps with a wiki system to gather maps and satellite images.

Wikis are designed to encourage collaboration by making it easy for non-technical users to add and make changes to the sites. They also allow users to share documents, deadlines, and communications. Since everyone in a group has access to the information, the sites are self-policing. Users can crosscheck it and make changes, which can be both good and bad. The openness is nice, but that means if you run your own Wiki, you'll have to monitor it constantly for accuracy.

Social Applications

Unlike typical applications, like word processing and spreadsheets that run on your own computer, social applications live on the Web or on mobile devices. What makes them social is that they involve any number of users and incorporate a social component. As an example, Plaxo is essentially an address book that allows users to update and share their contact information with their network. Get Satisfaction helps businesses offer customer support by building communities around a company's products and services. Squidoo is a site that makes it easy to create a page around a topic of interest, and then allows visitors to add their own ratings.

Applications may also take the form of plug-ins for browsers or widgets which may be added to a website. Lijit, for example, is a widget that allows website visitors to do a search of social sites.

Then there are those applications designed to enhance social sites. For example, hundreds of tools exist to support Twitter, such as TweetDeck, which is a kind of dashboard for managing an account. Onlywire helps share blog entries across other blog sites.

Finally, as we've seen, there are applications that help you create your own social network, like Ning or SocialGo. Bantam helps you create a private workspace for your team. Others offer social widgets you can integrate into your site, like KickApps and Google Friend Connect.

Your own applications

Developers are finding unique and interesting ways to make their applications social. Sometimes "mashups" are created by combining social functionality with certain features and topics for a specific community. Certain social sites, like Facebook for example, offer tools known as API's (Application Programming Interface) for building applications designed to work on their sites. This book obviously isn't about programming, but even without technical skills, you can take advantage of social tools to automate and enhance your operations, marketing and social participation by incorporating the ones that already exist.

There are plenty of websites that will help you create them too, including OpenSocial. Zembly allows you to create and distribute widgets and social applications for Facebook, Meebo, OpenSocial, and the web.

For those more technically inclined, whole business models can be built around a social application, or applications can be built to work with specific social sites or for use on mobile devices like iPhones.

What's a Widget?

A widget is a bit of software code that can be embedded in a Web page. It's often a tool of some kind created by a third party that allows a website visitor to interact with it, either to get information, do a calculation, play a game, or any number of things. Widgets are also known as modules, snippets, and plug-ins.

Applications may also be developed as third party add-ons to social sites. They can help you do a whole host of things, like integrating a blog into a social network (Blog Link) or helping people in a network share their travel plans (Tripit). Add-ons like these make social sites more sophisticated and useful.

Email: 1-to-1 and Narrowcast

Email should be considered part of the social media mix, because it helps extend the relationship beyond the originating social interaction. It takes several forms, including:

- Emails sent directly to an individual (1-to-1)
- Emails sent to social site groups
- Email notifications
- Emails you send to many at once, like newsletters (narrowcast)

Social sites allow users to send emails directly to people in their network, as well as to groups they belong to. Email notifications, which we'll address a little later, allow users to choose the types of communications they'd like to receive. Creating your own newsletters or other periodic communication is useful for deepening relationships with people you meet on social sites, that is, once you obtain their email addresses.

Narrowcasting or sending the same communication to a group or email list also can be an effective way to keep in touch with many people at once. Although not individualized, what you say is personalized (by name) with content that is relevant and meaningful to the reader. That makes it more effective. Email services, like MailChimp, ConstantContact or Vertical Response to manage these communications offer many benefits including widgets for capturing email addresses into a database, tools for creating emails and reporting. There's more to email marketing, which we'll see in Chapter 15.

Chapter 6: Properties – Your Digital Real Estate

Properties are basically the places on the Web you create and control, such as your website, blog or Facebook page. They're often the places a reader ends up after reading one of your social posts.

There's no requirement that you have every type of property, but a website is essential. An email signature is simple to create. Deciding which ones you need depends on what you're trying to accomplish and the level of build-out, administration, maintenance and marketing you're willing to do.

Although the overarching idea for all of them is promotions, some like your website achieve that objective more directly. Beyond the website, you can have a blog, Twitter page, Facebook page or YouTube Channel where you're responsible for creating most of the content. Others are useful for creating a "private" space where your network can congregate and engage, such as on a wiki or in a social network group. They're useful when you can encourage your network to create most of the content, but administration can be time consuming. You can also build sites to contain existing content or feeds, like on Squidoo. They let people share in your interests while you show off your expertise, and you don't have to do all the creating yourself. You will have to promote them to keep them active, however.

The following is a list of property types describing where their content comes from, for the most part. And of course, there are hybrids; you can always add feeds to your website, a Wiki can include your own material, etc.

Property	Your Own Content	User-Generated Content	Harvested Feeds
Website	X		
Email signature	X		
Blog	X		
Twitter page	X		
Facebook Page	X	X	
YouTube Channel	X	X	
Group		X	
Wiki	X	X	
Social network	X	X	
Yahoo Pipe			X
Squidoo Lens			X

There are many tools available to help you create the various types of properties. For a website, you could create one from scratch HTML or use a builder tool like Squarespace. You could also use a blogging tool, like Wordpress. This is a good idea if you want your own blog. If you need a place for a group to congregate, you could set up your own social network on a service like Ning or create a group on LinkedIn. A wiki can be created with Wetpaint. For the others, like Yahoo Pipes, visit their respective websites to set them up.

Chapter 7: Common Social Activities

Now that we've taken a look at the different types of social media sites, let's go deeper on the more common features, functionality and activities.

There are so many sites and applications, with new ones being created as we speak, that if you think of something you want to do, there's probably a tool out there that can do it for you. It's often a matter of visiting a site and clicking on every menu item to see what's available. Activities can include chat, messaging, email, video, filesharing, blogging, forums, discussion groups and applications.[41] Not every site has them all, but the idea is to make the most of the ones offered.

Build a basic profile

Upon arriving at a site, the user is typically asked to sign up and create a profile with the minimum of a user name and email address. The site uses this information as the visitor's unique identifier, tying all of their account information and submissions to it.

Depending on the site, profiles may be enhanced with any of the following:

- Links to websites, blogs and other properties
- Personal photos; sometimes with a caption or title
- Text about the user, like a bio or history, schools attended, business experience, etc.
- A logo
- Favorites things, like books, people, etc.
- A person's real name and gender

Beyond the profile, a user can go on to do any number of activities, depending on what the site allows:

Set Privacy, Email Notifications and Other Options

Once someone signs up, they can personalize their account settings. Account preferences may be set for all sorts of things, like email notifications, permissions about sharing content, and privacy in terms of who is allowed to view the information. Users can often choose the types of emails they would like to receive. These notifications can be about new members and their contributions, invitations to connect, etc.

Users can also edit their account settings, customize the look or layout of their pages, manage bookmarks and tags, edit social options, and integrate with their other social services, like blogs and Tweets.

Upload Content

Users can add content like images, video, animation, articles, event pictures, audio, podcasts or blog entries. It makes it more interesting for visitors and a reason for them to follow, stay, read and come back for more. When the material is original, it can demonstrate expertise, build reputation and generate buzz.

Socialize: Create Site-Specific Content

One of the easiest ways for users to get their feet wet is to leverage simple content creation tools offered at the site. Many of the following are typical of social networks. Any of these activities are usually associated with the participant's name, which provides exposure:

Wall posts This is the area where a social site's members can post short comments about what they're up to.

Lists Many sites allow users to create all types of lists, such as favorite books, music, websites, etc.

Review, rate, vote, share an opinion.

Q&A Asking questions or seeking opinions generates interactivity, which helps build relationships and awareness. Users can position themselves as experts by providing useful answers to questions. Many sites will allow people to rate the responses, and good ratings often bring the expert to the top of the page.

Events People can post workshops or seminars to drive attendance, or simply RSVP to show their interest in a particular topic.

Tags make comments or content searchable. Many sites allow users to select from a list of pre-existing words or to add their own.

Invitations and Joining Groups

Once someone has signed up and uploaded content, they'll want to get people to join their network. There are several ways to do this. Most sites let you invite people by name and email address, which can be uploaded or typed in manually. To expedite the process, there's usually an invitation template, which can be customized for the person or group being invited. Many also offer the option of searching the user's Gmail, Hotmail, Yahoo or AOL address books. To access this shortcut, the user can create an account on one of these free services, and then upload lists from their computer's address book to their chosen service. Once this is done for one social network, it can be reused for others.

Groups provide access to a larger community, beyond a user's own contacts, of people with common interests. Groups are useful for learning about events, activities and new developments. They can also offer a way to connect with influential people in the community, such as thought leaders, subject experts, highly active users and connectors (people with a big following or network).

Another benefit of groups is that they sometimes send periodic emails with a digest of member participation, activities and events. Group members can opt-in to receive them. Active group members will show up in these emails. It's a useful way to get your name in front of people on a regular basis, which helps to create top-of-mind awareness. Another use for those emails is to see the other groups that members are joining – you may want to follow up on these to see if they're right for you to join, too.

To find groups to join at a site, search by interest, industry, company, alma mater or association. As we've seen, many sites allow you to set up your own group property, as well.

Sharing: Links, Chiclets, RSS

Sharing information with a network is one way to start conversations and encourage interaction. It can also position the user as someone "in the know" or as a "subject matter expert," which helps keep people interested in what they have to say – which in turn may result in traffic to a website.

One way to share is to simply include links in comments or posts. Sites also offer tools in the form of sharing icons or chiclets, or through Really Simple Syndication (RSS is described later). Simply click on the icon of the site where you want to share your information, and follow the directions for connecting to that site. Depending on what is offered on the site you're on, these tools also allow users to subscribe to feeds, bookmark a page, vote for an article, or post a profile or blog. They're the easiest way to link one site to another one, so the same information doesn't need to be entered on multiple sites.

A selection of the icons representing various websites is shown at right. If you're not sure which site the icon represents, simply mouseover it; many sites will pop text that explain what they are.

There are so many social networks now, companies like Share-This and AddThis have developed single icons to represent many:

ShareThis.com AddThis.com

Website publishers employ these to make it easier for their visitors to share what they've found. The services also allow users to import their address books, which makes it easier to share content with the people they know.

RSS is another way to spread the news. It allows people to select information sources that interest them, whether that's a blog, podcast, videocast, etc. The idea is that it saves them from visiting multiple websites, because the information is delivered to their feed reader. A feed reader is software that aggregates content into one place for easy viewing. Bloglines is just one of the tools you can use for subscribing to RSS feeds. Some web browsers, like Safari and Firefox come with RSS readers. Another free tool may be found at Feed Reader.

Recipients can filter the information they receive by keyword so they can further customize their feeds. Feeds may also be used to monitor changes to a website. This could be especially helpful for users of Wikis, so members collaborating on the site know when the site has been updated. RSS feeds can help keep you informed about what's happening in your industry or with your competition. Local feeds can keep you up-to-date on news related to your business. A key benefit is that it can de-clutter your email inbox, too. Sign up to get a newsletter feed, rather than an email, so you can read it at your convenience via RSS.

Use RSS feeds for research to stay on top of your industry. If you're a blogger, it's a great way to stay up to date on topics you want to write about. You can also set up feeds to keep tabs on what people are saying about you or your business at social sites. We'll talk about how to create your own social media dashboard later in the book.

To get a feed, click on the RSS icon that typically looks like the one here and follow the instructions to add it to your reader.

For publishers, RSS can be a great way to distribute content. Some website platforms are already publishable as RSS. If you need to convert your content to RSS, you can use a tool like Dapp Factory.

The downside to RSS is that it's often more useful to website publishers than the vast majority of consumers who are unfamiliar with its benefits. Don't automatically expect website visitors to be interested in your RSS feeds. For the majority of consumers, RSS is a mystery.[42]

Make It Easy to Connect

If you want to get more people to visit, follow you or join your networks, let them know where you hang out. Add badges on all your properties, such as your website and print materials. Maybe add a few to your business card. Many sites offer little graphics and links for that purpose, like the ones for Twitter:

spoongraphics.com   milkaddict.com   mirkku.com

Add Events

Many sites make it easy for members to post and find events, RSVP, share events and more. Some even provide tools for setting up and promoting events to their memberships. More on this in Chapter 15.

Applications, Widgets and Gadgets

Many social sites offer users software applications, and small programs called widgets and gadgets, to make their sites easier and more fun to use. They also help to increase interactivity and engagement with the site. The applications may be games, puzzles, polls, sharing tools and more.

If done correctly, applications can spur positive interaction and involvement with your brand. People will also want to share them, and other websites may want to integrate them into their sites, which further spreads the word about you and your business.

Other types of applications provide users with a way to connect one social network with another. Facebook, for example, allows you to pull blog entries into your account, so every time you post on your blog, it will also appear on your page. Your network will be kept up to date and it saves you from posting in two places. Slideshare connects with your LinkedIn and Facebook networks. And there are many others that allow you to cross-pollinate.

For the more adventurous, you may want to find or create your own widgets from sites like WidgetBox or Clearspring. If you're a developer, or can afford to hire one, you may want to consider creating custom applications through an API or developer toolkit.

Try It Now

It's time to get your feet wet.

1. If you're not already familiar with the leading sites, check out Facebook, LinkedIn and Twitter. If you are, visit the sites and try something you haven't done before.

2. Proceed to visit at least two of each *type* of site to get a feel for what's going on in the social space. Check out GetSatisfaction to see how social media is being used for customer support. See Sources for more ideas.

3. At the sites, try out some of the simple features. Surf around, read an article, vote or review content. If you need to, create a simple profile with the minimum information. Review and set up your email notifications.

4. If you don't have one already, assemble a list of keywords. Try out Google's Adwords tool to help you.

5. Research something about your industry. If you can't find what you're looking for, submit a question of your own. If you're in a technical field, visit Technorati's tag cloud to see popular topics. Use Tweetsearch to find topics or people of interest. Go to Upcoming to look for live events you may want to attend.

6. If you're local and/or provide a service, check Yelp to see if anyone has written about your business. While you're there, check out the widget you can add to your website.

Part III: Social Strategy

Planning Makes Perfect
Target Audience
Communication Objectives
Social Media – One Choice Among Many
Knowing When to Use Social Media
The Social Media Plan

Chapter 8: Planning Makes Perfect

Well, maybe not perfect, but it will certainly help you avoid expensive missteps and crucial opportunities. A plan is a map for navigating to a goal at a specified future point in time. It describes where you are now and where you want to be – whether that objective is to acquire more customers, sell more product, increase market share, improve image, increase exposure, raise prices, etc. A clear path will prevent you from running in circles, wasting a lot of time and money, or missing a chance opportunity.

Planning is often skipped, because small business owners are so price sensitive and time-crunched that they want the magic bullet – the fast, cheap and easy way to get the word out. Rarely can you achieve all three. Owners often depend on word-of-mouth, but if few people even know about the business in the first place, there's little chance of that being successful. And if left alone, it takes a long time for word to spread. Laying a good foundation will prepare you to take full advantage of opportunities as they come along and actively promoting will get you to where you want to be a whole lot faster.

When it comes to social media, people often ask, "Do I need a blog?" "How often should I email customers?" "Should I be on Facebook?" And that's before they've figured out who their customers are. Maybe that's because social media is all over the news and if they don't get on board, they'll be left behind. They don't consider what it takes to make the medium effective; they just hear the success stories. Or they see someone else using it, but don't consider how their situation may vary and yield different results.

For social media to work, you need to know how it applies to your business. First and foremost, you need to understand your target audience – who they are, how they make purchase decisions, where they look for information, etc. Do they even use social media? Then you need to think about how you will use the medium strategically – what you want to accomplish with it and how it fits in with all the other options you have for promoting your business.

The social media plan isn't all that different from other types of plans, and it draws on all the plans that should come before it. These include the business plan, marketing plan and promotional plan. Often, there's a marketing communications and media plan, as well. See the chart on page 55.

From the business plan, we'll begin to understand the role marketing plays in the success of the business and the financial resources that will be devoted to it. From the marketing plan, we'll take product/service descriptions, target audience, competitive landscape, a definition of the unique selling proposition (USP) and budget allocation (i.e., how much will be spent on product development vs. promotion). The promotional plan describes the positioning, messaging and branding. The communications plan outlines more specifics on the what, when, where and how the target audience will be reached.

There are many books written on these topics. For now, we'll focus on those aspects that relate to the social media plan, which outline the:

Target Audience (Chapter 9)

Communication Objectives (Chapter 10)

Social Strategies (Chapters 11-13)

Tactics and Execution (Part IV & VI)

Measurement (Part V)

Chapter 9: Target Audience

Your target audience consists of the people who may be interested in purchasing your product or service, as well as those who influence them. Understanding who and where your target market is, what they care about and how they behave is the core of any marketing plan.

It's necessary to define your target market because you don't have the time, money or energy to promote to everyone, and through every social site. You need to be selective. And the resources you devote to marketing to a specific target audience will be used far more effectively and efficiently, because you won't be wasting them on people who aren't interested. I'm not saying that other people couldn't be persuaded to buy your product or service, but that effort translates into higher marketing costs. That's why it makes sense to go after the people who are already part way there.

Defining your target audience will also allow you to create messages that specifically address their needs and resonate with them, which is much more effective than diluting your message to a general audience. You'll be able to choose the right media, so they'll actually see your message, and time the delivery, so they'll get it as close as possible to the moment they're ready to buy.

Understanding your target profile will help you determine if social media is the right way to communicate with them. It may seem obvious, but you shouldn't be focusing much of your energy on social media if your audience isn't using social sites. They'll never see the information you post there. Or put another way, if they are using social sites, find the ones where they hang out. Whatever you can do to match your audience to the medium will give your social efforts greater impact and yield better results.

For example, if your target market includes seniors or the less Web savvy, there's a good chance you're not going to reach a majority of them through social media – at least not now. However, the world of social media is expanding so rapidly, its use may be as ubiquitous as the Web in the near future. For now, you may be able to reach those within a particular target market by focusing on the more Web-literate among them, like the Social Selectives we defined earlier.

Target profiles may be defined along the following dimensions: demographics, geography, psychographics and behaviors. As I've said, there are many books on the subject, but here's a brief explanation of what they are and their impact on social media strategy.

Business Plan			
Management	Operations	Marketing	Finance

Marketing Plan			
Customers (Target Audience, Chapter 9)			
Competition			
Product	Price	Place (Distribution)	Promotion

Promotional Plan			
Objectives	Strategies	Tactics	Measurement
Chapter 10	**Positioning** **Messaging** **Branding** **AIDA** Awareness, Interest, Desire, Action **TEMPS** Time, Emotion, Money, Personal Info, Sweat	**Promotional Mix** Personal Selling Advertising PR Sales Promo	

Social Media Plan			
Objectives	Strategies	Tactics	Measurement
Chapter 13	Chapters 11-13	Chapters 14-17	Chapters 18-19

Geography: Where is Your Target Market?

Your customers may come from around the neighborhood or across the ocean. The type of business often establishes the boundary. For example, most retail and service business customers are local. If you're a coffee shop, most of your customers come from the surrounding neighborhood or they're commuters. That means your first marketing expense is rent – you're paying to be in a particular location to be available and attractive to that audience. Your second marketing priority is signage, to make the most of the walk-by and drive-by traffic. A third priority may be to place coupons in customers' bags to encourage repeat business. While they're there, you may want to encourage them to sign up for a mailing list, so you can send them coupons via email or a service called Groupon. And on it goes. Notice, there's no real mention of social media. Not yet. Once you deal with the priorities, then it may make sense to see where social media fits in.

On the other hand, if you're selling a product through the Internet, your customers may come from around the world. In this case, digital marketing and social media makes more sense. If you're selling written material like a book, you may only be limited by language or culture, and therefore selecting social destinations in-language is the way to go.

Proximity and travel distance often define geographical limits for the business as well as the customer. This is especially true for service-type businesses where the delivery takes place at the customer's location (landscapers, plumbers, cleaning, etc.). For professional services, like consultants, graphic designers and accountants, it may be important to meet clients face-to-face. Unless the consultant is very specialized, it is unlikely clients are going to pay for travel, so the target area is defined by how far the consultant is willing to travel to meet the client.

A key advantage a small business has over a larger one is the ability to provide personalized service, which a large business may not be in a position or be willing to deliver. Large businesses need to stan-

dardize to economically manage a large volume of customers. Therefore it makes sense for the small business to focus on creating personal relationships with their local customers, which fits in nicely
with social media.

Although the Web has a global reach, there are many social sites
designed to meet local needs, like the Seattle Tech Startups wiki or
Yelp's city-based reviews. Hyperlocal sites, like EveryBlock,
Outside.in and Patch, narrow the focus even more down to the
neighborhood level. Geographically targeted social sites can help
limit competition from vendors outside an area, as well.

Consider the location of people in your personal and professional networks when choosing social sites. For example, you could
set up a Twitter page just for people in your area. When using social
media calendars, think about how far people will be willing to travel.
For an hour-long seminar, you'll need to draw attendees from a narrow radius. For a weeklong conference, people will travel farther.
Choose your social media calendars and sites accordingly.

Geography may also play a role in the number of people using
social media. Mainstream sites have bigger audiences in certain areas.
"Facebook is still more heavily represented in the eastern half of the
United States, particularly in the great Plains, when compared to the
overall online population. New York, Illinois, and Ohio are the top
three states in terms of share of traffic... ."[43] For more geographic
data, visit a site like Quantcast.

Geography may also help you gain a better understanding of your
customers. There are common characteristics and behaviors shared
between city-dwellers versus suburbanites for example – more singles
in the city; more families in the suburbs. "The last 20 years have
clearly shown that the location of an individual, a family or even a
business play an important role in the prediction of the characteristics of that individual."[44] One way to use the anecdotal information
found at social sites would be to determine where to expand or start
a new business, for example.

Geography also plays a role in how someone is going to make a purchase – especially if the need is immediate. If a customer needs it now, they're not going to wait for shipping. The Pets.com failure is a classic case. Often, people buy dog food when it runs out, just like they buy food for themselves. They weren't going to wait to make that kind of purchase, and they certainly didn't want to pay shipping on something as heavy as 10 pounds of kibble.

Demographics: Age, income, education and the like

Demographics define people by race, age, income, disabilities, mobility (i.e., number of cars, commuter time, etc.), education, home ownership and employment. Knowing the demographics of your audience will help you determine the most closely targeted social sites. If you're already in business, look to your existing customers to define common characteristics. For more information, define your geographic area, and then gather demographics by zip code, MSA (Metropolitan Statistical Area), city, state, etc. Good, basic sources of demographics are the U.S. Census or your local government's website.

Once you define your market demographically, you can look for social sites that match your target profile. Many of them focus on certain age groups, like BOOMj for Baby Boomers and Eons for seniors. Hundreds of sites have been created for kids and young adults and everything in between, like Webkinz, Club Penguin and Boom-Bang. If you're looking for consumers based on their income level, consider their interests, like looking for bargains or making smart purchases. These folks may be looking for sites that provide detailed information, which means that reviews and comparisons are more useful to them than lifestyle content.[45] If your demographic includes a certain educational level, you may choose anything from Classmates to alumni association sites.

Psychographics: What people are thinking?

Demographics, and age in particular, are just one aspect affecting social media usage. But these days, people are just as likely to find connections based on interests, which makes the psychographics of users that much more important. Psychographic variables include: personality, values, attitudes, interests, opinions or lifestyles.[46] Knowing what a customer thinks and cares about will help you understand their motivations and actions.

Psychographics and behaviors are what being social is all about; so defining your target profile along these dimensions is incredibly important to the successful use of social media. After all, it is a social medium. In some industries, like fashion, entertainment and cars, it's the most important factor of all. But it also has a big influence on the way people buy less-sexy products, like financial services and insurance. "While My Space and Facebook get all the attention, social media focused on topics as remote as knitting or bird watching can be a strong branding target these days. These more focused audiences should be popular with brands because relevance trumps size."[47]

Granted, there are certain interests that change as we age or progress through various life stages. Parents are a good example; generally people having babies and raising children will fall into a generalized age group. But travelers can be any age, although that age and income may determine how they travel. Another example is a person who's into tech toys. This could occur at any age, income (since prices have fallen) or education. It's more about the person and how much they love technology. So when marketing to someone like that, you wouldn't necessarily target by age alone. What you really want to do is select by what's in their heads – what they read, the websites they visit, the groups they belong to – that's the way to reach your audience when it comes to social media.

There's a whole world of niche sites that appeal to certain interests. In fact, long established Web communities have always had some level of social activity. Discussion boards and forums have been around since the early days of the Internet. Also, communities are creating their own social sites with tools like Ning and Meetup.

The review site TripAdvisor offers extensive travel and destination information – the majority of it provided by travelers themselves, which makes it social. They claim to have over 20 million traveler reviews, opinions of hotels, vacations and more.

TripAdvisor's demographics are interesting. Almost 50% of the site's visitors are 45+. About a third earn more than $75,000 per year. Over 65% are married. Doesn't sound like your typical social media user, does it? If you offer any type of travel service, this is probably one place you want your business listed and reviewed.

Behaviors: How do people act?

Understanding how someone behaves or purchases your product will not only help you determine which social sites to use, but how and when to make the best use of them. Consumer behavior looks at how individuals, groups, or organizations go about making purchases, which is a process influenced by several factors:

- Whether the individual is buying for themselves or within the context of a group (i.e., family) or for an organization (i.e., employee).

- By the type of product being purchased, i.e., a tangible good versus a personal service.

- Macro factors, like the economy, going green and health news.

- Timing issues, from seasonal buying patterns to knowing when someone has a specific need. Certain events in a person's life can trigger the need to buy something – from minor (running out of printer ink) to major (getting married).

- People are also highly influenced by others, especially when products are confusing, risky or difficult to compare or otherwise high involvement, like technical products or healthcare services.

They look to their friends for referrals to make their choices less complicated.[48]

Knowing your customers' behaviors will make your marketing efforts more relevant to the recipient. This in turn will make them more receptive to your messages.

Geography	Demographics	Psychographics	Behaviors
Neighborhood	Age	Beliefs	Usage occasion
City	Sex	Values	Benefits sought (quality, service, economy)
State	Education	Attitudes	
Zip	Income	Lifestyle	Price sensitivity
MSA	Occupation	Personality	Status
Region	Family size		Usage rate
Country	Family lifecycle		Loyalty
International	Home ownership		Readiness
	Religion		Attitude toward product
	Ethnicity		
	Nationality		

When Your Customer is a Business

Although business people are consumers too, they're affected by their *bizographics* as well as their demographics. This information includes things like their title, role and responsibilities. The better you understand the person, the business and their industry, the more effective your marketing will be.

DIGO Founder and Creative Director Mark DiMassimo, "More than ever you have to be valuable to an executive before the sale. ...Social networks allow a marketer to establish themselves as an essential resource early in the process, and therefore you can get on the short list of an executive when they consider who they want to do business with in the future."[49]

Business buyers aren't making purchases for their own personal consumption. They buy things to help their companies or their clients make money, reduce operating costs, or satisfy a social or legal

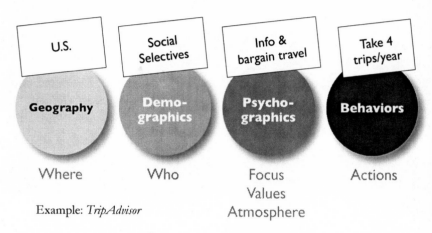

Example: *TripAdvisor*

obligation. The exception may be solopreneurs or very small business owners who often blend personal and business use.

Social media can play a part in the purchase decision, because buyers are going to look for trusted referrals, especially when the individual is looking for something they're not familiar with, a high involvement product, or they're making a costly or risky investment.

There's a big difference between marketing to an owner versus an employee, and it's crucial to understand this when you're communicating with a small business. When owners make a purchase, the expenditure may feel like it's coming out of their own pockets. This makes them very sensitive to price, so they're going to spend a lot of time shopping around. An employee isn't as sensitive, since they probably aren't feeling the pinch personally. In this case, making their job easier may be more important than price.

Small Business	Large Business
Marketing to owner	Marketing to employee (typically, unless you have access to the owner).
Price sensitive: feel the pinch	Relatively price sensitive: it's a budget decision and relative to other benefits, both personal and business-related.
Spend time shopping around (if they have the time)	May use standard bid procedure with several decision makers.
May not have expertise internally, so look for outside advice and referrals	May have internal expertise, but will look for outside advice and referrals when they don't or for high involvement products and services.
No restrictions on Internet access	May have policies restricting access to the Internet.

Knowing an individual's role in the company, the functional area, level of influence, seniority, responsibilities, and decision making power will help you communicate more effectively. Environmental, organizational, and interpersonal influences play a big part in decision making, as well.

The purchasing process for businesses is more involved than one for a consumer. It often requires vendor searches, RFP's, approvals, etc. In many cases, more people are involved and there can be a long sales cycle. You may need to apply to get on a company's shortlist before they'll even approach you for goods or services. Follow up and persistence in this case are crucial, and social media can play a supporting role here.

You need to understand the buyer's industry, how it operates and how their decisions are influenced by their position in the channel (supplier, manufacturer, wholesaler, distributor or retailer). Partner or personal relationships may also affect their buying behavior. This could be your starting point for choosing the right social sites, such as those related to industry associations, related businesses, vendors, etc. And consider the halo effect of being a member of the right organizations.

Companies are just starting to get in on social media and many have restrictions on where their employees can surf and the social sites they can use. Most likely, the larger the company the more conservative their policies are going to be. You'll need to take this into account when choosing social media for reaching your B2B customers.

Bizographics:

- Title
- Credentials
- Department
- Function
- Seniority/Influence/Power
- Responsibilities
- Industry
- Employees
- Revenue
- Locations
- Headquarter Location
- Seats (commonly used in the software industry)

Try It Now

Gather the following information from your business and marketing plans.

1. Your overall marketing goals.

2. Customer profiles by geography, demographics, psychographics and behaviors of consumers and the people who influence them. If you sell to businesses, create bizographic profiles.

3. Think about how your audience may be using social media (if they are at all). Check your website stats to see if you're already getting any traffic from social sources (see Chapter 18 if you don't know how to do this). Ask your existing customers if they're familiar with social media. If so, ask them which sites they use and what they do there. You're trying to answer the following questions:

   - Are my prospects or customers using social media?
   - What sites do they visit?
   - Why do they go to these sites?
   - What do they do there?
   - What do they contribute?
   - How often do they visit?

Chapter 10: Communication Objectives

The objective of communication is to alert, inform, engage, persuade and remind potential buyers of a business or product to influence their opinions or elicit a response as they move through the purchase cycle.

The purchase cycle describes a series of discrete phases that someone goes through before making a purchase, from first hearing about a company or product, to researching and evaluating alternatives, to actually buying it. Understanding what those steps are and what is going through the mind of the customer at each phase will help you decide which objectives will work with your audience. For example, if they haven't heard of you yet, you need to focus on building awareness. Once they get to know you, you'll need to provide the information that's going to convince them that you're the right provider. If you're selling a service, and people need to get to know you before they'll buy from you, you'll need to engage them in conversation to create a relationship first.

Before making the decision that social media is the right tool for meeting your communication objectives, you need to take a step back and consider your overall marketing goals. Are you trying to grow by adding more customers or selling more products? Will you sell to existing customers or try to acquire new ones? Will you focus on your industry or expand into others? How many customers do you actually need? What's your deadline for meeting these goals? Establishing clear objectives will help you figure out what to do to achieve them. As they say, if you don't know where you're going, you'll never get there. Your goals should be realistic and placed in order of priority. Write them down, and keep them in front of you so you can refer back to them when it comes to making marketing decisions.

The chart on page 69 outlines objectives typical of each phase of the purchase cycle. You'll need to determine which ones are relevant to your particular business.

As we've seen, social media can play a part in helping you achieve many of these objectives. Some would argue, however, that this is a cold, old school list espousing traditional corporate marketing ideals, not the new world where social media is about creating community and good will. Yes it is, but the business objective is to grow that community so it's interested in ultimately purchasing your product or service. That's really no different than a company donating branded T-shirts to the local little league – everybody wins. They're doing it for goodwill, yes, but also for the benefit of the company. Otherwise, they could just donate unbranded shirts or simply make a cash donation without recognition.

Rather than having an issue with the objective, what distinguishes social media from other types of communication is the way you go about it. We've talked about social media as a persuasion tool, not a sales tool. You shouldn't be selling to people on social sites. The idea is to attract or bring them to you by informing, enlightening, entertaining, inspiring, and yes, making them aware of you, helping them to realize what you offer and giving them a way to remember your solutions when they're ready to buy.

Try It Now

1. Document your prospect's typical purchase cycle. Consider what they think about, their decision making process, the websites and media they seek out for information and the people they speak with at each stage. Think about how influential they consider those sources and why.

2. Think about how long each phase may take and when they may occur.

3. Consider what might inhibit them from proceeding through the process – what might be their objections? It's important to anticipate them, so you know what to say to get them over the hump.

4. From the communication objectives provided, select the 2 or 3 in each phase that are most applicable to your business and audience.

Chapter 11: Social Media – One Choice Among Many

There are many ways to promote a business to achieve the objectives outlined in the last chapter. Knowing how to choose the right ones will help you put together the optimal combination, so you can communicate more effectively and efficiently with your target audience.

Promotional methods fall into four categories known as the *promotional mix* – personal selling, advertising, public relations and sales promotion – and is based on several theories. One is that using different methods to deliver a message increases the odds of the target audience seeing and internalizing the message. That's because people get information from various sources, and it's not always easy to identify which ones they're using and when – while some like newspapers, others prefer reading blogs. Researching your audience's media habits will help you determine what's best.

Certain types of information work better in different formats. For example, advertising is good for delivering brief, simple messages because it's limited to the space or time purchased. On the other hand, when a product is complicated, sensitive or requires more explanation, personal selling may be appropriate.

You should also consider a medium's impact, which is its ability to create memory and to stimulate action. Memories are the result of repetition and emotion, which depend on the medium itself and the creativity that goes into the message. Social media, which is subtle and varied, may not have the same kind of impact as, for example, an ad on television, which hammers the same message over and over in an exciting, multimedia format.

Advertising however is viewed with more skepticism than other promotional methods, because it's becoming increasingly obvious to viewers that there's an ulterior motive. The audience knows that an ad is from a company, not necessarily a trusted source. Advertising is considered to be "invasive to the overall experience unless [it's] transparent, unobtrusive, relevant, and entertaining."[50]

Of course, the level of skepticism depends on the person's prior experience with the company. On the other hand, social media itself shouldn't escape a certain degree of scrutiny, considering anyone at any time can write almost anything they want, which makes its credibility difficult to assess. In many ways, social media is like PR without an editor.

Personal Selling

Personal selling is person-to-person dialogue between buyer and seller, in person or by phone, and the activities that support it, such as prospecting, networking, presentations, meetings, training, incentive programs, sampling and telemarketing. This promotional method is used when there's value in meeting in person, when building a relationship is important to the sale, when deeper explanations or two-

Communication Objectives				
Alert >	**Inform >**	**Engage >**	**Persuade*>**	**Remind >**
Generate brand or product awareness	Explain how product or service is provided	Encourage interaction with company, brand or product	Drive trial	Create top-of-mind awareness
Increase name recognition	Suggest new uses	Create dialog between company and audience	Encourage brand switching	Remind customer where to buy
Develop reputation	Educate about the value of product/service	Increase audience conversations	Change customer's perception of product/service attributes	Get customer to refill/repeat order
Build buzz	Create a positive association (halo effect)	Get fans and evangelists talking	Influence buying decision	Increase stickiness
Build company image	Establish/regain trust		Get customer to take specific action	Build loyalty
Introduce or launch product/service			Drive foot and website traffic	Improve customer satisfaction
Increase search rankings			Generate referrals and leads	
			Establish partnerships and relationships	

Source: 2001 South-Western College Publishing; add others

* Not to be confused with the whole idea of social persuasion. In this case, it's simply a moniker for getting someone to take a specific action.

way conversations are needed, for complex products, and to deliver live demonstrations. Personal selling is labor-intensive and reaches only one person at a time, which makes it the most expensive promotional method. That's why it's important to give it the best chance for success by leveraging other elements of the promotional mix to generate leads and open doors for the sales call.

Social media fits in this category, because in some ways it can be used to build one-to-one relationships through networking and conversations. Demonstrations can be provided through slide shows and video. Expertise can be demonstrated by offering tips and helpful resources. But as we explained in the early part of this book, it's virtual, so it doesn't have the same punch as meeting someone live.

Live vs. Virtual

There are many reasons for going to live events. You may be looking for new contacts, to see old friends, to talk over ideas; you may be shopping for referrals, or intending to meet potential customers or investors. Sometimes you just want to go to an event, because you're tired of working in your home office alone. That's valid, but more of a personal reason – it could lead to business, but indirectly. The same is true online. It takes a lot of time and energy to go to an event, so be selective about the ones you choose to attend. How to choose the right social sites is discussed further in Chapter 14.

When Meeting Face-to-Face Makes More Sense

- You need to discuss a touchy subject.

- When non-verbal cues are important, as in cases where someone may not want say something directly.

- The conversation needs to be synchronous (a two-way conversation happening in real time).

- Providing reassurance is important.

- You want to do a show and tell or live demonstration.

- When the conversation may take a long period of time.

- You want to have a discussion as a group, like a brainstorming session.

- For making a more personal connection.

- Your physical presence is required, such as in photography or videotaping.

- Only meeting someone face-to-face will give you an idea if you can work with this person (as in an interview).

- Reporters are present, and you need to be there to answer questions.

Advertising

Advertising includes any paid presentation and promotion of ideas, goods, or services by an identified sponsor. It can include print ads, radio, television, billboards, direct mail/email, collateral materials (brochures, sales slicks, etc.), catalogs, signs, in-store displays, posters, motion pictures, Web pages, digital ads, etc.

There are more places to advertise than I can count, so you really need to understand what to use and when. That depends on many factors, including the media habits of the target audience, placement and production costs, coverage area, and how frequently it will be necessary to communicate with the audience to make the message stick.

When it comes to advertising, you'll need to select the appropriate media mix. Media includes broadcast (like TV and radio); narrowcast (like Internet and mobile); print (like magazines and newspapers); outdoor (like billboards and shopping carts). There's a lot of information out there on the pros and cons of each medium, as well as how to choose the optimal media mix, which is beyond the scope of this book.

Social media can be used to enhance the effectiveness of advertising. For example, social media interactions may be built into the ads themselves, like gifting, commenting, voting and games. They can help get people more involved with the advertising message. The idea is to get people talking about and interacting with the brand, rather than just passively viewing an ad.

Public Relations (PR)

If you're looking for a way to educate an audience, enhance your reputation, tell a complex story or deal with a sensitive subject, PR is the way to go. Unlike advertising, it's perceived as more credible because it doesn't seem like the information is coming from an advertiser (although it often is). And where it's published affects how it's perceived. For example, an article in the New York Times online is going to be looked at differently than let's say an article on Business.com. The former is likely more selective in what it places on its site.

PR can be a great way to leverage the power of mass media, without the expense of placement. However, that doesn't mean PR is free. The cost is in the preparation of materials and the time it takes to do the media relations to pitch or sell story ideas. If you do some of the work yourself you can reduce the out-of-pocket expense, but it still takes a lot of time, effort, knowledge and creativity, and perhaps hiring of professionals, to make it successful.

The way it works is that you prepare materials, such as articles, reports, announcements or press releases for the media outlets. In addition to telling a newsworthy story, the material you prepare needs to be well

Social media is like PR without an editor.

written and in proper format. Then it's a matter of contacting editors, publishers and producers to interest them in putting your "story" or whatever it is in their publications, on their websites or on the air. You don't have control over its placement though, because that's at their discretion. Their goal is to publish or air material of interest to their audience, because that's what increases their circulation or viewership, and that's what ultimately is responsible for the value of their advertising.

PR and social media are close bedfellows in that they're designed to attract attention, rather than sell. Social media has also become a new way for PR professionals to distribute materials, beyond traditional TV, radio and print. Plus, the viral nature of the medium extends its reach. "In the online space, all media outlets are now multimedia outlets, and with increased acceptance of visitor comments and user-generated content, they are quickly evolving into social media outlets. Publications once dedicated to delivering news in a print format now have the ability to compete with broadcast outlets with streaming live video, embedded audio and video clips and images."[51]

Publishing Options

If you have a story to tell, there are many options for getting the information published. The important thing to remember is to get your information in front of the right target audience. That means knowing where they are, what they're looking for, and understanding their preferred format (text, images, video, audio; short, medium, long).

	Where to Publish		
Properties	**Other Sites**	**Alternative Formats**	**Think**
Website	Related, local publications or by industry, affinity or community	Handout	What are they looking for?
Blog		Booklet/eBook	
Newsletter		Slideshow	Where will they find it?
Group	Directories	Teleclass	Preferred format?
Facebook Page	Blogs	Webcast	
Squidoo Lens	PR distribution	Podcast	What do editors want?
	Aggregators		

There are places you can publish without needing to get past an editor, including your own website, blog or newsletter. The material you create for one can be repurposed to work on another, which can save time and extend its value. However, in the case of your own properties, it's incumbent upon you to build an audience so the material gets sufficient exposure to be valuable.

Besides your own properties, there are other places that allow you to simply upload an article without editorial oversight. The beauty of publishing on other sites is that you're leveraging their traffic, which in many cases gives you exposure to new people who haven't heard of you yet. To find them, look for the option to "submit" on sites targeted to your audience.

You can also upload materials to sites that "aggregate" articles by topic, such as Creative Commons or ArticlesBase. Another option is the online distribution service, like PRWeb or PR Leap, where you can post press releases. Basically, these services share your information with media outlets, and they provide a place where journalists and editors can find stories. The value of these services has been questioned, however, because anyone can post anything. This makes them a less credible place for journalists to source stories, which may limit how much they use them.

Key differences between advertising and PR:

- With advertising, you pay for the space or time. With publishing, you pay with time and professional expenses.

- Advertising lets you choose the where and when. Publicity is at the discretion of the editor, although if you deliver the information at the right time, you have some influence over the when. And who you send it to, or your media list, influences the where.

- You create the advertisements to fit the medium's format. Publishing allows you to influence the format and length of the material to some degree, but it's still up to the editor to decide what actually gets printed or aired.

Advertising	PR
$	"Free"
Bold	Subtle
Shallow	Deep
Skeptical	Credible

Sales Promotion

Sales promotion is about providing incentives that stimulate the purchase or sale of a product, usually in the short term. It's useful for time-sensitive promotions. It can include coupons, sweepstakes, contests, product samples, rebates, tie-ins, premiums and trade-ins. These may be delivered offline or online, through kiosks or at events.

There are many ways to tie these ideas to social sites, and surveys have shown them to be effective with social participants. As an example, microblogging sites may be a good place for announcing sales and specials, because messages can be delivered via mobile and at

Promotional Mix	
Personal Selling	Prospecting, Networking (live, virtual), Presentations, Meetings, Training, Incentive programs, Sampling, Telemarketing, Phone calls, Personal correspondence (letters, email)
Advertising	Print (newspapers, magazines, yellow pages, newsletters, advertorials, etc.), Broadcast (radio, TV, etc.), Collateral (business cards, brochures, flyers, posters, sales sheets, T-shirts, pens, PDF's, slideshows, podcasts, etc.), Direct Marketing (snail mail/email, direct TV, catalogs), Environment (signage, merchandising), Internet (websites, linking, search, etc.), Narrowcast (Internet, mobile marketing), Out-of-Home (billboards, shopping carts, digital signage, movie theater, etc.)
Public Relations	Press kits; Press releases, announcements, articles and reports; Distribution via print, electronic, digital and *social* media; Media Relations; Events (trade shows, open houses, exhibitions, seminars, webinars, etc.); Charitable contributions, speeches and issue advertising
Sales Promotion	Coupons, Sweepstakes, Contests, Sampling, Rebates, Tie-ins, Premiums (T-shirts, pens, bags, desk toys, etc.), Trade-ins

specific times; coupons and contests may be included in an email newsletter.

New Definitions of the Promotional Mix

Marketers have been trying to redefine the promotional mix for years by slicing and dicing existing concepts. *Direct Marketing* lumps snail mail, email and websites into one idea. *Relationship Marketing* concerns personal selling and customer support, particularly as it relates to services, rather than tangible products. *Digital Marketing* covers everything Web, from pay per click advertising to social media. More recently, *Word-of-Mouth Marketing* that aims to get consumers to provide information to other consumers. WOMMA, the related organization, is including social media, too.

Some might say social media should even have its own place in the promotional mix, but I think of it as another medium. Sure, there are different ways to handle it, but that's just as true for other media. Where it eventually lands in the promotional mix, however, will be up to the marketers that implement it. According to a recent survey by the email marketing company, StrongMail, social media is emerging as a direct marketing channel. "… there is still a wide-spread land-grab for ownership of social media within the various facets of marketing, with 29% of respondents stating that responsibility is owned by multiple departments. However social media appears to be emerging as a direct channel with 36% of survey respondents stating that the direct marketing department owns social media. Surprisingly, only 9% of the respondents report that social media is owned by public relations departments, suggesting that marketing teams value social media more for its demand generation potential than awareness building. A paltry 5% have a dedicated social media department."[52]

You probably don't have "departments" so from a practical standpoint, it doesn't really matter where social media fits in the promotional mix. What matters is that you recognize where it belongs in your overall promotional plan, along with all the other options available. And that you don't get sidetracked by all the marketing pundits who try to tell you their way is the only way to market.

Chapter 12: Knowing When to Use Social Media

Social media is more or less appropriate depending on many factors including the type of product, the audience and their behaviors, the promotional mix and not least of all, your available funds. What I'd like to concentrate on are the key features of social media; where it works well, where other media might make sense. Then, through a process of elimination and a review of the tradeoffs, you'll be able to arrive at the optimal promotional mix.

Type of Product

Characteristics of a product or service influence how it should be promoted. This includes its nature, where it's sold, its price point, and how frequently it's purchased.

Dog Biscuits vs. Pet Sitting

Marketing intangible services requires a different approach than the one used for tangible goods. Intangible means a buyer can't see, touch or try a it before they buy, so it's up to the marketer to provide evidence that the service can be delivered with some reliability. This "proof" may be visual, like a portfolio (client list, case studies, publicity, testimonials, references, awards, licenses, etc.), printed material and website; and educational, like an explanation of the process for providing the service. Some of that evidence may be delivered via social media in the form of informational conversations, materials (slideshows, videos, diagrams, images, etc.) and publicity.

Many services can only be delivered locally, but social is global, which means you need to find local ways to use social sites. More on this later.

Timing communications appropriately is important with intangible goods, because they're often "perishable." If you hold an event, for example, once the date of the event passes, the inventory is gone. The same is true for consultant hours, cab rides, hotel rooms and many others.

Services sometimes involve making a big sale or hitting a long-term contract, not selling a big volume of units every week. That means the purchase cycle may be a long, slow process involving several decision makers. The payoff can be big, but communications need to sustain over a longer period.

Level of Involvement

Evaluating products and services can require a certain commitment on the part of the buyer. It's what marketers call "level of involvement" or how much time and energy someone is willing to give to the purchase decision. That investment depends on many factors, such as how complex, confusing, expensive and risky a particular purchase is. For example, a low involvement product might be something like a tube of toothpaste. It's readily available (say from a local grocer), inexpensive and can be easily replaced with something else if the buyer is unsatisfied for some reason. The risk is low in that there are few if any consequences if the buyer makes the wrong choice.

High involvement products on the other hand are complicated or confusing, expensive or high risk. Consider the difference between buying a toaster (low) versus a refrigerator (high). An individual is going to spend a lot more time evaluating the high involvement product, especially when it's a big-ticket item, like a home, car or trip. High involvement goods may require a business to build a relationship with the prospect first, because the buyer's perceived risk needs to be reduced before they'll purchase. There needs to be a certain level of trust.

Services, like those provided by consultants, hair stylists or doctors are high involvement, because engagements may last for a long time, can be expensive, and there's significant risk if the provider doesn't do a good job. Services are often difficult to evaluate before they're performed, so people seek out more information. Educational materials, information from third parties, referrals and recommendations are very influential in this case.

When the risk is high, referrals have more impact on the buyer than advertising. For this reason, personal selling, PR and social media can be more effective in influencing the perceptions of a potential buyer. An advertisement for a dentist may be looked at with some skepticism and carry very little weight, but an article in a respected magazine will. There's little risk in purchasing chewing gum seen in an ad. Even a recommendation from a total stranger on a review site will have more impact, because the reader assumes the reviewer has no vested interest in sending more clients to the dentist. With this in mind, you'll want to make sure your happy customers are saying positive things about you on social sites that matter. It can also mean getting the industry pundits or media sources to put in a good word for you.

There are several cases where social media has played a role in successfully promoting low involvement products too, but they seem to be ones with features that embody a customer's allegiance – what might be called a high social affinity with the audience. Guinness for example ran a campaign to get users to sign a petition to make St. Patrick's Day an official holiday.[53] Bacon Salt is another good example, where two "regular guys" from Seattle found 37,000 people on MySpace who claimed they loved bacon, connected with them and became a success.[54] Let's not forget though that this story is as much about finding the right product for the right market, as much as using social media to connect with them. What's interesting, particularly in the case of Bacon Salt, is that results seem to come a lot faster and be a lot bigger than slow-burn high involvement products or services. It could be that it's simply an easier product to get ones head around.

Product Lifecycle

How and where you promote often depends on the product's lifecycle, which is comprised of the introductory, growth, maturity and decline phases. At the macro level, the product lifecycle is concerned with the product category or industry. At the micro level, it concerns a company and its products. For example, motorcycles are macro; Harley Davidson is micro. Social media may be used at every stage of the process.

Introductory Phase: When a new type of product is launched, it's unfamiliar to most people, so the whole category and not just the product itself, needs to be promoted. People need to be made aware that it exists and educated about what it does. New technical products often experience a longer introductory phase, because information about them needs to pass through several types of people – from innovator to early adopter – before they achieve traction.[55]

We can apply a similar idea at a micro level. In other words, if you're a new company, you need to build awareness and name recognition for your products and services. However, you need not market the category if it isn't new. You need only focus on why your particular company is the best choice for the buyer among all the other options available (see Zen Marketing).

Advertising and public relations are typically used for creating awareness at this early stage. They are the fastest way to communicate with a large number of people in a target audience. Sometimes paid advertorials are used (a combination of advertising messages and editorial). Promotional materials, like printed brochures and websites allow for deeper explanations.

Using social media to create awareness will take longer, unless you have a product or service that catches fire on the social scene. That could happen because it's a really exciting product or the marketing campaign itself is innovative. That was the case for Cadbury-Schweppes' unknown Stride chewing gum. The company sponsored a massively successful and a little bit strange viral online video called "Where the hell is Matt?"

Growth & Maturity Phase: As the product category matures, more companies enter the market and competition intensifies. People are more familiar with the category, but now need to know which product to buy or why they should by from a particular company. They need to be persuaded that you're the right choice among many, so it becomes important to emphasize what makes you better in terms of what the customer cares about. This is known as differentiation or differentiation value in marketing lingo.

You can create points of differentiation in your products, pricing, distribution and promotion by being contrarian. Do what your competition isn't doing. Find new channels of distribution to get exposure to new customers – this may also limit competitive pressure because you're available where your competition isn't. Use advertising, PR and social media messages to communicate what makes you different. Use niche media channels that haven't yet been discovered by your competitors, and talk about yourself in unique and creative ways. You can also use sales promotions, like contests and offers, to stand out from the crowd. The more you're differentiated, the less you're a commodity, and that means you can become a preferred provider (and most likely charge a premium over the average price in the market).

For people familiar with your services, you need to maintain top of mind awareness – people need to be reminded that they should continue to buy from you. Using your mailing list to communicate directly with customers is very appropriate here. Social media is also a good fit, because it's inexpensive to communicate frequently. Plus, many social sites require that people become members of your network or follow you – they're already fans, so reminding them that you're around is relatively easy to do.

Product Lifecycle and the Promotional Mix

	Intro	Growth	Maturity	Decline
	Heavy advertising (if budget allows) and PR	Advertising and PR to promote brand loyalty; emphasize differentiation value	Decrease ad spend	Decrease in ads and PR or stop
	Sales promotion to induce trial		Increase sales promo	Limited sales promotion
	Personal selling to establish distribution		Support existing customer base	Divert existing customer base to alternatives
				Reinvent product/find new market

Proximity, Volume and Purchase Frequency

Effective communication reaches its audience closest in space or time to when they intend to make a purchase. That's why shelf location and product packaging is so important in a supermarket. Consider the value of placing products near the cash register for the impulse purchase. Or, consider the ads for candy and popcorn at the movies. You'll also want to think about how frequently someone makes a purchase. There's a big difference between buying a home and replenishing paper towels. The same idea may be applied to social media. You'll want to participate in sites when and where your audience is thinking about a particular topic related to your business. Your audience may be frequenting Facebook to touch base with friends and family, but when they're looking to buy a car, there's a good chance they're visiting a shopping site for reviews.

Your business model is relevant, too. For example, there are many companies that rely on a volume strategy, earning low margins selling many units. Sales promotions, like bulk discounts, are typical when it comes to getting customers to buy a lot at once. Another way to achieve volume is to get customers to buy repeatedly and frequently, and that depends on the type of product. Consumables like food and paper goods, for example, often need to be replenished. Staying top-of-mind is important here, too, so customers are reminded to make repeat purchases. That can be achieved with package stuffers (combined with some type of incentive like a coupon), direct marketing (if you have the buyer's contact information) or frequent advertising (can you say fast food?). Once again, social media may have a role here, because it's cheap and easy to achieve frequent messaging.

For many types of businesses, such as home remodeling or pool installation where purchases repeat very infrequently, the "repeat purchase" comes in the form of a referral. As we've discussed, referrals are very important for services. Before social media, the business would either need to ask for a referral or hope that the customer would pass the word on. Now businesses like these can spread-the-word with content sites to show off their work and review sites for gathering testimonials to build awareness and reputation.

Target Market Characteristics

As we've said before, understanding your target audience is essential for effective marketing. An exploration of the following characteristics in relation to type of product will help you further in choosing the appropriate promotional vehicles to use.

Consumer or B2B

The first consideration is whether the product or service is designed for consumers or business customers. As we've described earlier, each has their own needs, desires, purchase behaviors and influences. When it comes to choosing media, you need to understand their media habits as well – what they read, what they listen to, the social sites they participate in, what is more likely to influence them.

If you're not selling direct to consumers, you'll need to consider the various groups you need to communicate with throughout the channel. For example, you may need to persuade a retailer to carry your product as much as you need to persuade the end consumer to buy it. This is what is known as a push/pull strategy. You're pushing your product out to the retailer, and pulling the consumer into the retailer to ask for the product.

Geographic Dispersion

If your market is concentrated within a specific geography, it's easier and probably a little less expensive or time-consuming to reach them. For example, if you know that people select a place to get a workout based on a certain distance from where they live or work (because if they go somewhere on a regular basis, they're not going to want to travel very far out of their way), you can promote within a fairly narrow radius. That means you could advertise in a very local publication, get mentioned in your chamber of commerce newsletter, use local search engines, or participate in a neighborhood social site to reach them. Advertising on these sites is going to be a lot less expensive, because the media you choose will reach a smaller audience.

Level of product knowledge

As discussed previously, if your audience is unfamiliar with the category of your product because it's early in its lifecycle, you need to promote the category first. There are pros and cons to this strategy. Being first in the market means there's little direct competition. The downside is that you need to spend more time and money educating the market before you can focus on promoting your product. This is very difficult for the typical small business, because all that educating can be quite expensive. Hopefully, you've decided to operate within a well-understood industry or you can find some way to make your product more familiar by riding the coattails of something people already understand. It's a lot easier to focus on what makes you different within a category, than trying to persuade someone that they need the category in the first place.

Degree of brand loyalty

Some people only buy well-known brands; others could care less. And then there are those that develop an undying loyalty for a certain brand. Apple is one of those. Achieving this level of brand love isn't easy for the small business, especially in the short-term, because it can take a lot of money to get established. There are exceptions of course, as we've seen with Bacon Salt and Stride Chewing Gum.

Available Funds

Your budget will absolutely dictate what you can and cannot do in terms of promotions. Advertising is often expensive. PR is time-consuming. You may not be able to offer promotional pricing if you have thin margins. Personal selling can take a lot of your time or require you to hire salespeople.

The money you spend is in an inverse proportion to your time. If you have more time than money, you can bootstrap by doing the promotions yourself. Use online tools to automate and save time, like those for building a website, sending emails, managing your social participation, blogging and others. Learn how to write, or work out a trade agreement with associates to get the job done. Educate yourself about marketing (you're doing that right now!).

Your investment in social media will depend on your skill set as well as your pocketbook. For example, if you're a writer, keeping up with a blog may be easier for you than someone who isn't. If you need to hire someone to write the blog for you, that increases its cost. Do as much of the work as you can yourself, then hire professionals when you need to.

Allocation

Choosing to use social media is not an all or nothing proposition. Here are some things to think about when working social media into your promotional mix.

Synergy

Synergy is the idea that the whole is greater than the sum of the parts. When it comes to media, there are combinations that work quite well together because their characteristics are complementary.
Try combining:

- Magazines, which have a long shelf life, with a higher frequency medium such as radio, out-of-home (i.e., billboards, shopping carts) and social networking.

- Radio with a visual medium like TV, print or out-of-home.

- Out-of-home with a more detailed medium such as print or Internet.

- Internet with a visual or mass reach medium like print, out-of-home, TV or radio.

- Advertising and editorial into an advertorial format.

- Mass social networking sites, like Facebook, with niched ones like TripAdvisor.

Synergy also considers how people receive information, and it's not always a linear relationship between the media and the recipient. That's why a combination of media at various times and in different ways gives your message a better chance of getting through.

In addition, balancing low- and high-cost options can help stretch your marketing budget, without sacrificing reach (the number of people in your target audience who get your message).

For these reasons, you may want to mix it up. If you're looking for sales leads, for example, you could do one or several of the following. It all depends on what is going to give you the best result.

- Purchase a list, then send out a mass mailing. Or you could cold call that list.
- Attend an event and hand out a lot of business cards.
- Mix live and online events, with social activity follow-up.
- Write a press release and get it published in a newspaper.
- Run an ad in a trade magazine.
- Search a social networking site to find names and ask for connections. Or locate your contacts and expand on the relationships.

Tradeoffs

With all the hype it's getting, people often reach for social media first when it comes to marketing. However, if your goal is to build awareness about a new product, public relations is probably a better way to go. Let's do the math. You could spend a couple of weeks posting to social sites, say 2 hours a day, to reach a few thousand people in your social network. Maybe they share it with 2 people each. You've just spent 20 hours to reach about 6,000 people if you're lucky. Or, you could spend about the same amount of time creating a press release and putting it up online. If you're lucky in this case, that press release will not only get picked up by a few websites, it could get reprinted by a local newspaper that reaches tens of thousands of people. That's a lot more efficient than spending hours and hours connecting through social media. Not only that, you won't be waiting as long to see results. Of course, this is a very simplified example. There are too many variables involved, but hopefully you get the idea. And of course, you could do both. But if you want to build awareness more quickly with a large audience, get the press release done first. Then you could leverage social media to extend its reach to online calendars, your Facebook page, your website, blog and more.

ROI

How you allocate your resources among all the options will depend on the expected return. Put your money and your time on the ones that get you the best result. If a certain percentage of your business is more likely to come from say yellow page advertising, you may still want to use social media, but limit your investment in it.

Opportunity Cost

Your investment in social media is for the most part measured in the time it takes to participate and the money you pay someone to help you with it. The value of that time is measured by its opportunity cost – the value of the other thing you could be doing instead. Rather than hanging out on Facebook, you could be writing that press release we talked about. We see the same thing when a business focuses all their energies on driving their names to the top of search engines. Sure, in some cases, this is a good strategy, but not always. Consider keeping a record of how much time you're actually spending on social media, so you can see if using your resources on another medium would be more effective. For many, making a sales call or writing in a blog may be a better use of their resources.

Experimentation

Sometimes the only way to figure out if social media is the right way to promote your business is to make an educated guess about what might work, then measure the results and tweak the formula. This is especially true if you have no history with social media or any other promotional methods for that matter. There isn't a big risk in adding social media to the mix, since it has such a low out-of-pocket cost. However, be selective in how you choose which ones to use and how much time you invest. Narrow down the options, then experiment. We'll provide more information about how to do this in Chapter 14.

Try It Now

1. Describe your product in terms of the types discussed and list the relevant characteristics. Think about where you are in the industry and product lifecycle.

2. Think about your business model and how many actual units you need to sell or the number of customers you need to acquire.

3. Based on the communication objectives you chose in the last exercise, give some thought to the different promotional activities you can undertake to drive prospects along the purchase path. Consider the ones you would choose if social media weren't available. Conversely, think about how social media could enhance or replace some of the techniques you've been using.

Chapter 13: The Social Media Plan

If you're still reading, you've probably decided that social media fits somewhere in your promotional mix. You've taken a look at how to allocate your marketing resources. Now we need make a plan for social media, from setting objectives through the tactics that will help you achieve them. This means defining how audience, medium, message and timing come together.

Social Media Objectives

The connection among communication objectives, like increasing awareness, improving image, generating goodwill or changing attitudes, and specific social media objectives, like gaining exposure, increasing engagement and building buzz isn't always clear. And it's even more difficult to track social activities like creating a profile, inviting people to your network, Tweeting or blogging back through all these steps to a specific sale. But having objectives is still important, because you need to have something to shoot for and a benchmark to see if what you're doing is working. And although social media is difficult to quantify and measure, they do have some measurable properties, as we'll see in Part V.

For the most part, social media takes its objectives from the public relations playbook:

Exposure

Exposure defines any opportunity for a reader, viewer, or listener to see and/or hear your message in a particular media vehicle. It may also be defined in terms of reach, or the number of people who see a message, website or other entity. The number of times they get the message, which is known as *frequency*, may also be factored into the equation. Gaining exposure is a matter of choosing media that attracts the greatest number of people in your target audience.

Engagement

Gallup research shows that engagement is comprised of confidence in the company/brand, belief in the integrity of the company, the pride that comes from association with the company/brand, and passion for the brand.[56]

When it comes to social media, the level of that engagement is measured by the number of people viewing and interacting with the content on a blog, website or other entity. It shows how interested someone is in the information. Theoretically, the deeper the interest, the more likely they'll be driven along the purchase path.

If your overarching objective is to increase engagement, because you believe that it will build trust in your brand and reputation, your social media goal may be to increase the number of blog or article comments, positive reviews or votes.

Word of Mouth (WOM)

WOM refers to the passing of information from person to person using any type of human communication, such as face-to-face, telephone, email, or text messaging, and now, any number of social media tools. It's measured by how many times the information is shared or hyperlinked, and at what speed (see page 94).

Influence

Influence is the effect someone has on an individual's thoughts or actions. This is at the heart of social media's power. There are several types of influence defined by the experts, but one is known as identification. It occurs when someone who they like and respect, such as a famous celebrity or a favorite uncle, influences a person.[57] The level of influence depends on the relationship, level of knowledge and the information being sought. Think about it. Who's advice would you take if you needed a new doctor – your mother or some celebrity? If you had a specific problem, maybe only a doctor's recommendation will do.

Influencers fall into all types of categories, including family (spouse, child, parents, in-laws), friends (old and new, high school, college, fraternity/sorority, grad school, work, etc.) acquaintances and business (boss, employees, colleagues, vendors). Geography plays in as well. Social site friends can be near and far, but whom do you call when you want to go to the movies? And how much influence do friends of friends have? There's a lot of research going on right now about the influence of online friends. "One San Francisco advertising company, Rapleaf, carried out a friend-based campaign for a credit-card company that wanted to sell bank products to existing customers. Tailoring offers based on friends' responses helped lift the average click rate from 0.9% to 2.7%. Although 97.3% of the people surfed past the ads, the click rate still tripled." The company "follows the network behavior of 480 million people," and one finding from this friendship data was that "borrowers are a better bet if their friends have higher credit ratings. This might mean a home buyer with a middling credit risk score of 550 should be treated as closer to 600 if most of his or her friends are in that range… ."[58] Imagine that. Social media could one day influence your credit score.

How you become a person of influence depends on your relationship, the perception of your authority and the value you bring to your audience. It's measured by the number of people who are interested in what you have to say, such as network growth, the number of people who invited you to join theirs, number of blog readers or followers, subscribers and the number of times you're quoted or referenced in conversations. It may also be measured by who is following you – being tracked by other influential people boosts your value.

Reputation & Image

Reputation and image in the marketplace is comprised of an audience's beliefs, ideas and impressions of a company.[59] For many industries, reputation is everything. This is especially true for high involvement products and services. Consider how valuable a good reputation is for a lawyer or financial professional.

However, "…a handful of bad reviews is worth having. 'No one trusts all positive reviews,' says John McAteer, Google's retail industry director for shopping.google.com. 'So a small proportion of negative comments—"just enough to acknowledge that the product couldn't be perfect"—can actually make an item more attractive to prospective buyers."[60]

Tracking the quality of conversations and how fast word spreads is especially important here. Using your judgment, you're looking to see whether the comments are generally negative or positive. And again, you're going to want to look at the authority of the person talking about you.

Viral & Velocity

Viral Growth measures how many people shared your information online, where it's being shared and who's getting it, indicating how relevant or important it is to people and their networks.

Velocity refers to how fast your information spreads to other sites and where it has gone. The speed at which it moves, and whether it's rising or falling, can indicate how relevant or important the information is.[55] IceRocket offers a tool for measuring velocity. Klout has data on Tweets.

Buzz

Buzz is an elusive concept, but it's one of those things – you recognize it when you see it. It's been defined as the excitement surrounding a brand, incident or idea that spreads via word of mouth or by going "viral" – when it's spread digitally via messages or links. The ability to create buzz is another story. Sometimes it's simply the instigation of a controversial topic, an age old debate, a mystery or talk about something in short supply that everybody wants.

Buzz is one way to see what's hot and what's not, and there are many companies trying to figure out how to capture this elusive entity by monitoring conversations. I'd say there's much more to it than simply tracking keywords, but Facebook for example has Lexicon, which follows language trends on profiles, groups and event Walls, counting the number of times a word or phrase appears. Other tools include Google's Zeitgeist PR tool and Nielsen BuzzMetrics' Blog-Pulse.

Social Media Objective	Definition	Measurement
Exposure	Being seen	reach x frequency
Engagement	Connection	viewers x interactions
Word of Mouth	Person-to-person communication	sharing
Influence	Affecting thoughts and actions	network growth, invitations, followers, quotes, subscribers
Reputation/Image	Perception	quality of conversations + velocity + authority
Buzz	Excitement	shares + links + velocity + authority
Website Visibility	Website awareness	search engine rank + link popularity + website traffic

Website Visibility

A key objective of most communication strategies is to drive traffic to a website. One way to do that is to increase its visibility, so online searches result in awareness followed by visits.

Inbound links (links from other websites to yours), particularly from high traffic sites or well-respected ones that influence your

Put a Number on It

Marketing is often thought of as being rather squishy when it comes to measuring ROI. However, business is about numbers, and there are many that can be used to set goals and evaluate marketing's effectiveness. Consider increases in revenue (dollars or units sold), client acquisition or an X% increase within a specific period.

Goals are the benchmark against which you can measure results to determine if what you're doing is working and worthwhile. They can be set for each stage of the purchase cycle, from the number of people who first hear about you to how often the phone rings to the final sale.

audience, are one way to measure visibility. First, because linking from a respected site to yours lends credibility. Second, being seen on high traffic sites means you're leveraging their ability to attract and market to a large audience. Third, links from high traffic sites can get you higher search engine rankings.

There are many ways to acquire them, including asking for reciprocal links (you link to me, I link to you), adding your name to directories, publishing articles, advertising and through social media activities.

Getting directory listings, like yellow pages, may be as simple as adding your information in the appropriate places. For example, I have an industrial client on ThomasNet. Many allow free listings. The most important directory of all is DMOZ – first of all, because it's one of the oldest on the Web. Secondly, many online directories take their information from it. You'll want to be on Google local as well.

If you've optimized properly, which means the strategic placement of keywords in a site so search engines can find and rank it, your site will show up on search engine results pages. Where you show up on SERP's is one way to measure website visibility. The objective is to appear within the first three pages, because studies have shown that most people don't explore beyond that. However, that may not be easy for some small businesses to achieve and maintain without expending a lot of resources. That's why achieving top rank on search engines shouldn't be the only objective.[61]

SEO and SEM

Search Engine Optimization (SEO) means structuring a website and building in keywords in such a way that it increases the likelihood that search engines will find it.

SEO is one aspect of Search Engine Marketing (SEM). It also includes other Internet marketing activities designed to attract search engines, like getting inbound links from high traffic websites or paying for search advertising.

Strategies: Purchase Cycle, AIDA and the TEMPS Index

Paying attention to your customer's purchase cycle is one way to be strategic. Another way is in the application of the AIDA concept, which stands for:

A = Attention or Awareness
I = Interest
D = Desire
A = Action

AIDA defines what you need to do at each phase of the cycle to influence and drive prospects through it. The "A" represents awareness. Providing information and education creates interest. Engaging and persuading prospects develops desire and moves them to take action. The following chart shows which aspects of the promotional mix work best for AIDA:

Awareness	Interest	Desire	Action
Let them know you exist or get attention	Tell them what you do	Explain why they should buy from you	Get them to take action

	Awareness	Interest	Desire	Action
Best Promo	PR Advertising	PR Advertising Personal Selling	PR Advertising Personal Selling	Sales Promotion Personal Selling

The concept can play out in a specific communication as well, like in an advertisement. It serves as a guideline for its creation, providing a logical progression for the viewer's behavior. In this case, the "A" stands for attention, and unless you grab it, the viewer is never going to get the rest of the ad. Interest involves providing details about what you do in the body copy while supporting the headline. You'll also be making the case for why the viewer should desire you. Asking the reader to take a specific action is usually at the end.

When communicating, it's important to understand where your prospect is in the purchase cycle and the action you can expect them to take. For example, you'll bypass building awareness with existing customers, because they already know you.

When it comes to social media, however, it may not always be clear where they are, because users are in control of what they do at those sites. You're not in charge like you would be with an email sent to a specific person or an ad placed in a very targeted publication.

When choosing the Internet for building awareness, consider this data from Nielsen, "The Internet poses an interesting marketing conundrum. It is both the least effective of the three screens for commanding attention and building awareness, and the most effective in the latter stages of selling—powerful in its ability to persuade viewers to take action."[62]

The tactics you undertake can address several stages of the cycle at once. For example, answering a question on LinkedIn may generate awareness if people reading it haven't heard of you before. On the other hand, for those who have heard of you, it may encourage them to choose you over someone else. The important thing to remember is that prospects move through these phases at their own pace and in their own way, but it's up to you to provide and shape the

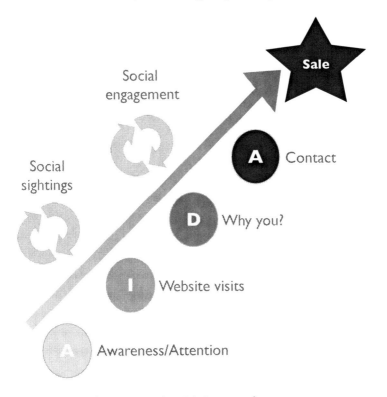

information at each stage so that it's in your favor.

Timing comes into play here, too. How long someone lingers at each phase depends on the types of products they're purchasing – not everyone is ready to make a purchase right after hearing about you for the first time. High involvement products require a relationship be created between the buyer and the seller before there's enough trust for the prospect to feel comfortable enough to make a purchase.

The following outlines the information you could provide at each phase (for more ideas, see Chapter 15).

Awareness or Attention As we've discussed, advertising and public relations are often used to generate awareness, because they have the potential to reach a large number of people at once. Despite social media's somewhat sketchy record of being able to effectively build brand, it doesn't mean you can't try to build awareness of your products and services with it as we've seen in the cases of Bacon Salt and Stride chewing gum. Place articles in magazines, online, in your blog or at high traffic websites. Share your expertise through question and answer areas on social networks. Post comments about some-one's article, which may also encourage a visit to your website. Place videos on YouTube to attract attention.

Unlike advertising, which can be very expensive, you can repeat messages everywhere without having to pay each time the informa-tion appears. Public relations is similar in that you can create a press release, put the information out on a newswire, where it may get picked up by several news outlets or websites. If the information is good and newsworthy, it could have a somewhat sustainable impact, which means it's not something you do every day typically. However, participation in social media needs to be even more frequent than PR, because as fast as you post something, there are thousands of other messages coming right after yours to compete for your audi-ence's attention.

Interest Explain your business and your products. Be compel-ling. Show that you understand the prospect's problem and make the case that you can solve it. Talk about features and benefits in terms of what's important to them. Make the short list. After awareness is achieved, they'll typically visit your website – be sure it's ready.

Desire At this point, the prospect is interested, wants more detail and will start comparing purchase options. You'll need to explain why you're the one to buy from, because you can satisfy their needs. They want to know that the company has been successful implementing solutions with other customers in similar situations. You need to demonstrate that you have the best product/best value and are credible/reliable. Differentiate your products and services from those of your competitors using demonstrations, testimonials, client lists, white papers, case studies, success stories, etc. Place them on your website, in an article, tell your story through a video or slideshow, answer questions on social networks, etc.

Action At this point, you want to lead the customer to take an action, which will depend on where they saw your information. For example, if you're running an ad to build awareness, the action you want them to take would be to visit your website, call you, send you an email. This is known as a *call to action*. Give a reason to act quickly, such as a deadline, expiration date, or limited availability, i.e., limited time only, only 3 seats left, sale ends Friday. Offering a coupon, particularly with an expiration date, is a common way to get people motivated. In social media, your call to action may simply be to get someone to visit your website after reading your post. You can either choose to communicate this blatantly, as in "visit my website for more information" or your information will simply be so compelling that they will want to follow up.

AIDA		
Objectives	**Strategies**	**Tactics**
A	Build awareness; create name recognition	PR, Advertising
I	Educate audience about features and benefits	Website, collateral...
D	Demonstrate quality, value, performance; improve image	Branding; photos; sampling, case studies...
A	Encourage immediate purchase	Discounts, coupons, limited time offers...

The TEMPS Index

I originally introduced the TEMPS™ Index on my blog as a way to describe how a website visitor might move from low to high engagement on a website, but it's a good way to evaluate the response someone might make to social media marketing.

Social media by its very nature is more of a relationship-building tool than a sales tool. That relationship is formed through a series of engagements between yourself and the participant in a fair exchange, which will help drive them through the purchase cycle.

The TEMPS Index measures a visitor's willingness to commit. A higher TEMPS means the buyer is more involved – the very definition of a relationship. Your goal will be to provide what's needed to raise the stakes as you move them along the purchase path.

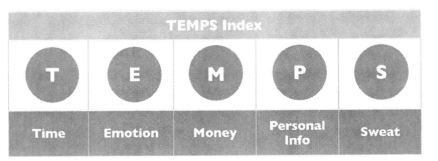

Time Literally the amount of time it's going to take the visitor to perform an action. Less time means a smaller perceived level of commitment. Time becomes less of an issue as the visitor's overall perceived value increases. There's a difference between getting someone to watch a thirty second video versus a twenty minute one – once they believe that what you say is of value, they're more likely to want to spend more time with you.

Emotion Represents the desire to be more involved. It's where making a personal connection with the visitor becomes so important. Really knowing your prospects – their psychology and behaviors especially – will help you express the right style and tone, which in turn helps create emotional attachment.

Money If you're asking for money – in other words, if you're trying to get them to make a purchase, you need to understand that price and perceived value are integrally related. In other words, whatever I'm buying better be worth it. And if it isn't a tangible product, but rather information, for example, it needs to come with a compelling reason why someone should pay. Applying the idea to social media, it can be measured in terms of social capital, which is the value that is derived from a network. This only works for people who connect with people selectively. If they connect with anyone who asks, then the connection doesn't have much value. On the other hand, an invitation from a person who is choosy about whom they connect with is more valuable, and ranks higher on the Index.

Privacy Depending on the behavior of the user, some people are really hesitant to provide personal data. Even on social networks, there's a limit. For example, asking for income data drives the Index even higher.

Sweat Apart from actual time spent, this is the effort a visitor has to expend. It includes: thinking, sourcing information, typing, signing up in order to post on a blog, uploading content, responding, etc. The more trouble, the more sweat.

When the TEMPS Index is low, there's little at stake for the visitor – they don't have to give up any information, and they don't have to expend much effort or time in doing so. Asking a visitor to vote is a fairly low TEMPS request. Commenting and sharing an article is a little more involved. Higher activities include signing up for an RSS blog feed, embedding a video or creating and uploading original content. This will give you an idea of how it may apply to social media and your website:

You'll need to offer social participants something of sufficient perceived value to get them to want to give of their precious attention, time, effort and information. The higher their TEMPS, the more you'll have to give. The idea is to offer something that doesn't cost much, but has high-perceived value. Don't expect much without offering something in return.

Read Blog	Post Com- ment	Visit Website	Sign Up	Send Invite	Make Contact	Buy
Low TEMPS						**High TEMPS**

Let's look at the relative weights of these low and high activities:

Low	**High**
Read Tweets	Follow
Read blog	Sign up for RSS feed
View and rate video	Share or embed in their website
Visiting your website	Bookmarking on StumbleUpon
Viewing an online calendar	RSVP'ing for an event

When offering up your own social content, start by thinking about the actions you'd like your reader or viewer to take. Do you want them to visit your website? Sign up for a workshop? Read more of your articles? Save you to their favorites? Contact you? The higher the TEMPS, the more compelling your information or offer needs to be. Given it takes a number of touches to influence someone, providing them with content relevant to their needs will help accelerate the cycle, in addition to helping build a relationship with you. Here are some ideas:

- Downloads of information not available elsewhere (i.e., white papers, research, articles you've written, etc.)
- Access to resources (i.e., links, descriptions, etc.)
- Event updates (i.e., via a newsletter)
- Membership only access
- Community (i.e., social network)
- Permission to participate (i.e., in a blog)

- Promotional opportunities (i.e., sale notifications)

Using the right words might even be enough to persuade someone to take an action. We'll talk about how to do this in Part VI.

Zen Marketing

It's really Judo marketing, but I like the Zen of it. Judo is about taking advantage of someone's movement and momentum to drive them in the direction you want, rather than fighting it. All you need do is influence them to go that bit further. The Zen of it is that you're going with their flow.

In other words, you should focus your marketing efforts on those people who already are leaning towards a solution your product or service provides. Rather than selling the category, focus your marketing efforts on why yours is better. It's simply too expensive and time consuming to do otherwise. In other words, don't spend your time convincing a vegetarian that they should eat meat. Better to use your time convincing a meat eater to buy your particular brand of sausage. Applied to social media, you'll want to choose sites that already are attracting customers that believe in what you have to offer.

The Right Types of Sites

One of the first strategic considerations is to determine which sites you're going to use and participate in. I go into this in more detail in Chapter 14, but I'll touch on some of the main ideas here. First, it's a matter of knowing your capabilities, your audience and a site's reach. If you're not into creating original content, for example, you may not want to use a social content site. Next, you need to be where your audience is, so they'll see your messages. Then, the number of people visiting and participating at a site has to be high enough to make it worthwhile.

Choosing a particular type of social participation and site could be the basis for an entire strategy. For instance, to highlight your expertise, you may create a series of videos and post it to your own channel on YouTube. Or you may choose to build widgets and applications to position yourself as an innovative developer on Facebook.

You may also want to take advantage of the halo effect, which describes how someone's perception is influenced by prior experience or context. Of course, we're talking about the positive halo effect here. Association with the wrong sites or people can have a negative impact, too.

In traditional media, the halo effect is a big deal. If your article appears in the New York Times versus, say your local newspaper, you're not only going to get a lot more readers, but the association with a national newspaper brings you a lot more credibility. The same could be true for the social sites you choose, although to be honest, there isn't much proof of this and the effect could be fleeting as explained by Michael Hirschorn in an article from the Atlantic, "MySpace once enabled a remarkable social renaissance: Because of the site's indefinable halo effect, you would answer e-mails you would normally never open, meet people you'd never suffer otherwise ("Bill O'Reilly" is one of my MySpace friends). It was, in fact, not unlike freshman year at college. But what's remarkable soon becomes ordinary. MySpace remains cool—thanks to surprisingly deft stewardship by its new owner, News Corp.—but nothing is cool forever. And once the tantalizing pull of millions of people you could possibly be best friends with wears off, you're left with some by now pretty ordinary functionality: blogging; instant messaging; photo, video, and audio uploads; networking tools. Thanks to the inexorable process of Web innovation, such stuff goes from 'OMG' to 'Whatever' in no time flat."[63]

When it comes to social media, the halo effect may be more of a consideration for choosing a person to associate with, rather than a site per se. Sponsoring, responding to or getting the attention of a respected industry leader may provide credibility and exposure.

Another consideration is the idea of low-hanging fruit. There are literally thousands of sites and probably several dozen ways you can participate. You can't do it all, so you have to prioritize. We'll talk about how to choose the specific sites later, but the idea is to participate in the places where the most people with the greatest need or interest in your product or service are hanging out.

Social Branding

You may recall that a brand is a combination of experiences and communications that make up what a consumer thinks of or feels about a company, product or entity. Social media can be used to provide consistent messages and visuals to build on the brand you've established for your business and to reinforce the brand promise.

Messaging is a list of key points or ideas you'd like to convey about you and your company. Strategy comes first when developing your company's messaging. You need to know what motivates your audience, understand your competencies and what differentiates you from the competition (in terms of what your audience cares about), and your positioning. The idea is to put all that across in the best possible light. In other words, you need to come up with statements that speak to these concepts. When it comes to using these messages in social media, you need to reinforce them without sounding like you're selling something. The key concepts should be consistent, but shouldn't be said the same way every time; otherwise, they'll have a false ring to them. This is pretty much the opposite of advertising messages.

A company's brand is represented in the marketplace by its messaging and visual identity. The latter is the visual representation of the brand. It can include logos, fonts, colors, photo and illustration styles, and the like. Certain social sites allow you to customize your profile and pages. MySpace is well known for having a completely flexible layout. Twitter allows you to select a background image and colors.

You'll also need to figure out the style and tone you would like to portray. Offering up a little bit of personality, without making a complete ass of yourself, can be a good thing for building a brand. The idea is to find a balance between the risk of exposure, with its accompanying negative effect, and expressing yourself and your company in a unique, and perhaps revealing way, so you're interesting and memorable.

From a strategic standpoint, consistency and repetition work over time to establish a company's social brand. As people read more and more of its material, they'll start to develop a comprehensive picture of the company. By integrating your communications in this way, people will come to know you for the kind of information you provide, your sense of style, and what you stand for. This in turn will help set the expectation the next time they read your post, and you may get them to follow you regularly. In other words, they'll start looking for you, sign up for your newsletter, or they'll become loyal to your website. These are all good things, because they'll start coming to you, rather than you seeking them. It's attraction versus selling. By becoming a marketer, rather than a salesperson, you invite interaction, rather than always having to look for business. And people who are looking for you are already qualified prospects.

Apply the Strategies

Taking into consideration the concepts outlined in this chapter, here are some ideas for how social media can be used strategically. Which ones you choose will depend on your situation, and combining them in unique ways may provide an additional point of differentiation.

Make People Aware of Your Existence

- Combine social media with other PR and advertising activities to build brand, product awareness and website visibility.
- Make it easier to find your information and boost website visibility by including searchable keywords in content, and by tagging contributions.
- Use selected social networks to develop business relationships and to drive referrals.
- Boost search rankings by participating socially in high traffic sites and growing your link popularity.
- Use automation tools to distribute your information across social sites, build your audience, increase readership and get more exposure.
- Invite people to your networks to make connections, grow your community, establish partnerships and build relationships.
- Link your name, company name and/or product names at every point of contact.

Let Them Know What You Do

- Build brand by repeating messages and customizing communications wherever possible with visual identity components (logos, badges, colors, fonts and images).
- Associate with industry leaders, spokespersons and respected sites to take advantage of the halo effect.
- Enhance your social profile by using consistent language to clearly explain what you offer.
- Create original, compelling, educational material to demonstrate expertise and to build your reputation.
- Demonstrate your differentiation value in your content.
- Respond to questions in social network Q&A's, and participate in discussion boards and forums to show your expertise.

Get People More Engaged and Talking About You

- Consistently provide original, interesting, relevant and engaging content that gets read and shared (and make sharing easy).
- Use widgets, badges, games, polls and other devices to increase social interaction.
- Create an emotional connection by taking creative risks with your content – offer controversial or provocative material; voice your opinion.
- Provide useful industry information, not just information about your company, to sound less like a sales pitch and more like a helpful informant.
- Build social tools into your website to increase user-generated content, interest, engagement and repeat visits.
- Give fans and evangelists special treatment to encourage contributions and positive conversations.

Get Them to Take Action

- Hit the right frequency: get your message out there often enough to increase phone calls or Web visits.
- Stimulate immediate action through the use of sales promotions.
- Invite people to your network or group, or start a group of your own.
- Ask for recommendations, feedback and referrals (tell people what you're looking for).
- Consistently provide links to your properties to encourage repeat visits.

Remind Them That You Exist

- Participate frequently to maintain top-of-mind awareness and remind people what you have to offer and its value.
- Locate and participate in targeted groups to leverage the emails they send to their members.
- Provide frequent updates to keep your name in front of people (but don't overdo it to the point of being obnoxious).
- Encourage stickiness by developing or leveraging interactive tools, like games or surveys.
- Use simple social networking tools, like voting, reviews, comments, etc., to keep your name out front.

Try It Now

1. Prioritize the social media objectives important to your business.

2. If you're already participating in social media, take a reading of how you're doing in terms of the objectives outlined. Take a stab at quantifying what you'd like to accomplish. Remember, it's not an exact science.

3. Think about the actions you expect from the people you're communicating with. What will you offer in return?

4. Revisit the list of promotional activities you chose in the last exercise. Think about what you should do in terms of the purchase cycle, AIDA and TEMPS. Create your own list of activities for each stage. Choose a few from the lists I've provided; add a few of your own.

Part IV: Campaign Management

Social Site Selection
Promotional Activities
When It Makes Sense to Pay
Strategic Timing

Chapter 14: Social Site Selection

The first step towards making the most of social media is to select the right sites to use according to your goals, capabilities and target audience.

Sites by Type and Capabilities

As we've discussed, there are all sorts of ways to participate in social media. Knowing your own abilities and the impression you're trying to make can play a big part in the types of sites you choose. There's a big difference between creating original content and simply participating – for example, posting a response or voting is much different than writing an article. If you're a creator, that is you have the time, talent or inclination to create original material, content sites are a good choice.

Whether you choose to be a creator, a participant or a blend of both depends on your strategy. Certain types of businesses are a natural fit with particular social media categories. For example, a speaker might post a video on YouTube, list events in online calendars, like Yahoo's Upcoming, and upload presentations to SlideShare. If you're low on budget, but long on talent, that may help you decide. Writers may choose blogs; videographers may choose content sites; social animals may choose networks; subject experts may choose Q&A's.

Knowing when to take advantage of another website's traffic is important, too. For example, if your website, blog or other property doesn't get much traffic, participating in someone else's that already gets a lot of traffic makes more sense. Otherwise, you'll be spending a lot of your time and energy promoting them. If you have no readers, there's no point in writing. Unless your business model depends on content, this may not be the best way to go.

Targeting

Next, you'll want to find sites that match your target profile. The first decision is whether you need sites that primarily attract consumers versus businesspeople. In some cases, you'll need both, but for different reasons. The former, if you offer a consumer product or service. Add the latter, if you're looking for business customers and/ or referrals.

Mainstream vs. Niche

Before explaining how to find sites, I want to address the differences between mainstream sites, like Facebook, which attract a large, generalized audience, and niche sites, that aim for a particular audience by geography, interest, demographic, activity or affinity. It's kind of like the difference between network TV and cable. Facebook and LinkedIn get lots of traffic, but if you're trying to reach seniors, you won't reach them there. Better to go with a social site aimed at that demographic, like Eons. A balance of mainstream and niche may be the best strategy, since many social media users use both. "The one exception is LinkedIn, where the users are less likely to come from another social networking website."[64]

Mainstream sites don't usually go deep on specific topics, reach influential people in a specific industry or address a particular geographic area. However, they do reach a vast number of people, because they're more about the functionality they deliver than the subject matter (i.e., Facebook for social networking, Yelp for reviews, Stumbleupon for bookmarking, etc.). And once they gain traction, there are more people to invite ever more people to them. The media hype doesn't hurt their growth rate either.

The fact that they're so big hurts your chances of being seen amongst all the other people there. You end up competing with lots of message *clutter*. For example, Facebook gives you the opportunity to reach a tremendous number of people, but your message could get lost in all the activity – and quickly be forgotten. To get any kind of traction, you need to up the ante on participation, and be a consistent, creative and frequent contributor or advertiser. On the other hand, you could choose a niched site. Granted, the numbers won't be as big, but they'll be more targeted. With less activity and participation on the network, you get the opportunity to stand out among people who have an affinity with you, are more likely to see your message and care about what you have to say. Niche sites may not be as well known or attract the same numbers, but they'll reach your audience in ways that a mainstream site can't (unless you can find some way to attract a niche audience to a group on one of those sites). It's a matter of quality over quantity.

Browsers vs. Buyers

There's also speculation around the idea that targeted, niche sites are better for attracting people who are in the mood to make a purchase, because they're looking for product-specific information. Participating there may put you in proximity to an actual purchase. Many mainstream sites are more about hanging out with friends, so they're better for building relationships and creating buzz.

There are several ways to find niche sites that your audience and the people who influence them frequent. The best ones will both cover the subject matter and have high traffic. You'll also want the ones that attract a good amount of activity – that means they have quality content (and people creating it), high caliber participants, marketing and the tools that make it easy for visitors to share information.

Style and Substance

When looking for appropriate sites, make sure they're focused on subjects of interest in a style that appeals to your audience. The right people will be attracted to it and they're more likely to engage with the site frequently. To find these types of sites, look for media entities with an online presence, such as magazines and TV shows. You may also consider industry associations, networking groups and vendors that cater to your audience. Think about where your colleagues and customers look for information.

Once you've narrowed down the sites by subject, take a more in-depth look at them to see what the audience is talking about and what they expect to get from them. Listen in to see what questions they're asking, so you can see how you can make a contribution. If you're a realtor, it may not be cool for you to hang out on a travel site, simply because you think it matches your demographics. You need to have something relevant to say. If not, you could actually end up alienating people. Better to find the sites where you're a good fit.

Consider looking for local social sites. Geography can create an immediate affinity with certain audiences. Some people like to support businesses in their communities. It can be especially important for a service-type business to reach a local audience, because the service either needs to be delivered in person, or traveling a great distance is impractical. In addition to their online presence, local sites often host their own live events, too. That can be great for your business if it's important to meet face to face. As we talked about earlier, combining live and virtual networking can be more effective than virtual alone.

To find sites within a particular geography, include local magazines, newspapers, and radio and television stations that incorporate social tools. You can do this by adding a city name or other location to your searches. Meetup may be a good place to look, too.

You'll also want to look for sites that share information automatically with other sites, which makes it easier for you to spread the word. For example, Upcoming's event calendars are shared with many other sites.

Real Estate Guy

A twenty-something real estate guy approached me recently after I gave one of my talks on social networking. He wanted to know which site he should be using to promote his business. It's a question that's difficult to answer without asking a few questions of my own. "Among all the real estate agents out there, what makes you different?" Well, it turns out that he also did mortgages. Plus he was young, which might help him with new homeowners – they would relate to him. So I asked him what would trigger a young person or a first time buyer to have an interest in real estate. If you guessed getting married or having children, you'd be right. At this point, we had our answer. Find social sites that appeal to people looking for advice and information about getting married. Off the top of my head, I thought of The Knot. As it turns out, the site has a section on real estate called The Nest. With that in mind, I sent him off to check out that site and to discover parenting sites on his own.

Reach & Frequency

Once you've created your list based on content, you'll want to prioritize the sites in terms of the numbers of people they reach and how frequently they get your message.

Reach is the percentage of people in your target audience who are going to get your message. Your goal may be to communicate a message to 30% of the Soccer Mom's in Seattle. To do that, you need to figure out where they go for information; then put together the right combination of media that will get you closest to that goal.

Not every medium or social site will be targeted to 100% of your audience, unless there's a Seattle Soccer Mom publication or website out there somewhere (there could be!). So you need to understand how much of each medium touches your audience. For example, women may make up 80% of a general parenting magazine's readers, but only 2% may have children who play soccer.

Each medium has a different name for how they measure audience. For print, it's circulation. For radio, it's coverage area. On the Web, it's visitors, viewership or eyeballs. For social media sites, we might use the same criterion as a website, but we'll want to look at members, followers and groups, as well. Media measurement isn't an exact science, yet publishers and media entities base the value of their ad space or time on those numbers. It's up to you to determine a social site's value by matching those numbers to your target profile.

There are several tools to help you do this, but don't take the numbers literally; just use them to rank the relative value of each site. Some offer media planning tools for matching sites to your selected demographics. Some suggest related sites to ones you've chosen. Several offer toolbars you can add to your browser, so you'll be able to see the number of visitors when you surf to a site. Most of these work best for larger, more trafficked websites, but they're worth checking out in all cases because you can get a lot of data for free:

Alexa
Compete
Quantcast's Planner
Google Ad Planner
Google Trends
MSN adCenter Labs

What you're looking for is overall traffic, demographics and geographic dispersion. Page views per visitor and time spent on the site are good indicators of engagement.

Remember, the important numbers are the ones that show how many people fall within your target profile. With mainstream sites, you have to go a step beyond the big number to see if they're relevant. Look for ways to segment the audience by group, interest area, geography or other criterion. Often, the site will tell you how many members are in a particular group, but you may not be able to get a breakdown for the other areas.

Frequency is the number of times someone sees your message. In terms of online display advertising, one view is called an impression. And advertisers pay per impression. When it comes to social media, the cost isn't related to the number of times a message is delivered. That means you can build up a lot of frequency, without paying for each impression. This frequency has a lot to do with people remembering you, because as I've said, it takes repetition to create a memory. However, the messages aren't repeated verbatim, and social media messages need to be varied and subtle, so it may take more of them to create as deep an impression as an ad. On the other hand, hyperlinking and sharing increases the repetition and amplifies the message across the Web.

You also don't always know when the audience has a need to refer or purchase, so the frequency helps you build top-of-mind awareness and your message is more likely to be delivered when they're in the mood to buy.

Determining the reach and frequency of social media allows you to set numerical goals, which gives you a concrete target. The numbers allow you to measure the effectiveness of your participation and to make useful comparisons, although the results of course are open to interpretation, as you'll see in Part V.

Site Swag

Choosing the right sites to participate in can depend on what you're allowed to do at those sites. Many offer a chance to gain exposure and links just for the taking. Start by looking in the header and footer navigation for these free promotional opportunities:

- Directories to list your company
- Blogs to comment on
- Press release submission
- Q&A

- Forums or discussions
- Article, video, photo, etc. submission
- Event postings
- Opportunities to speak

The Case of the Interior Designer

Let's go through this thought process with an interior designer client of mine who is trying to drive more traffic to her website. Here's her situation and the materials she has on hand:

- Design expertise
- A beautiful portfolio and a number of awards
- A couple of articles written
- Several scheduled speaking engagements

Now let's take a look at the information we have about her target profile:

- High income earners, but could be retired
- Interested in contemporary design
- Live in the Seattle area
- Married, possibly Empty-Nesters
- Make design purchases in the Spring and Fall

Let's break it down by category first. We can immediately eliminate a blog, because she doesn't have the time or inclination to do much writing. Videos could be a great way to show off her work, but are too difficult and costly to develop at the moment. We'll have to stick with her still images, but they could easily be converted to a slideshow to put up on Slideshare or a similar tool. Since she provides a service, review sites like Yelp are a good idea, which also targets by city.

It's also important to think creatively about finding sites that appeal to her target audience. Although she's looking for people interested in interior design, they may have related interests like travel, wine and golf. They may also be grandparents. Participating in these sites may set my client apart from other designers; the trick will be to communicate in a way that connects the dots between these interests and interior design. In other words, an interior design article would be out of place on a travel site, but discussing how and where to display souvenirs may be appropriate.

For mainstream social networking, Facebook makes sense because of its consumer focus, but it will be useful to narrow it down on that site to groups targeted by her demographics and interests.

General contractors often refer interior designers, so adding business sites to the list makes sense, but not LinkedIn in this case, which targets managerial professionals. Twitter makes the list for announcing articles and awards, which may get picked up by journalists. For other followers, she could post design tips on a regular basis. And I would post her speaking engagements on Upcoming. However, before firming up these recommendations, I'd want to be sure her target profile uses these websites. I'll do that once I figure out the appropriate niche sites. Here are the steps I took to find them:

1. Used Quantcast's Planner tool and plugged in my client's demographics and geography, along with the "home decor & design" category filter. The top sites by affinity included: Better Homes & Gardens (BHG), Hometime, Martha Stewart and Taunton. The only freebie on BHG was a forum, but I imagine there are loads of advertising opportunities. Hometime and Martha are about the same. That's the issue with the larger sites; they're not giving much away for free. Taunton publishes books. So all in all, not as useful as I thought it would be.

2. Searched "interior design" on social media directories. I found many sites for students and other professionals – not the right audience. Ning showed how many members were in each social network and how many joined lately, but many weren't very active. But then I found *Zabitatz: Inspiration for Your Home*, which had

Where to Find Niche Sites

- Industry or neighborhood associations, networking groups, online media (magazines, TV shows, radio programs, etc.), vendor websites

- Alexa offers top sites by category, related site suggestions and more

- Look for the social media guide at Mashable

- Findasocialnetwork

- Socialnetworklist

- Ning

- When all else fails, type "niche social sites" plus your keywords into a search engine

878 members, but only 8 joined in the last month. ViroPop had 2,561; no members joined in the last month, but 8 photos were added. Okay, not too promising. At findasocialnetwork, I found *Curbly, a site for DIY'ers.* It had 5,764 members. I also found *30Elm,* but it seemed to be out of business. Socialnetworklist didn't return any results. Blog Catalog turned up *Decorati, Interior Design Ideas,* and *EhomeE.* There were many interior designer blogs, such as *Interior Design Resources & Budget Decorating.* I saved these for future reference for when my client had some extra time for posting comments. Then, since it sounded like a magazine, I checked out *Decorati,* because media-related sites are likely to have bigger audiences and participation than blogs. According to my Compete toolbar, there were 13,318 visitors. Much more promising.

3. To find more local sites, I narrowed the list with the following search query: "'interior design' magazines seattle." That turned up *Seattle Homes and Lifestyles Magazine,* where I found an event calendar and a blog to comment on; and a link to *Seattle Magazine,*

which had blogs, but they were off-topic and basically a directory of remodelers, which I imagine came with their advertising packages. I saved this for when we were ready to do PR.

4. I used the sites World-Newspapers and AllYouCanRead for a more general search. I found *Dwell*, *Architectural Digest* and *Contract Magazine*. Dwell, a consumer magazine, seems to attract the right audience. I circled back to Quantcast to check the audience profile, and it was showing about 2,000 visitors from the Seattle area. Opportunities for marketing include: advertising, blogs, project and event submissions, blog tips and a place for a client to submit a review.

I figured my list was more than my client could handle at this point, but I didn't want to leave any rock unturned. So I went to the Washington State listing of associations and found the *American Society of Interior Designers*, *Interior Design Coalition*, and the *International Interior Design Association*. These sites are more useful for industry connections, which are better if you're looking for referrals, rather than direct customers. I put these aside for the time being.

So here's my list so far with number of visitors and associated demographics:

Site	Visitors (Compete)	Demographics (Quantcast)
Upcoming	142.3 million This could be all of Yahoo, not just Upcoming.	Female, young adult, less affluent. Female is good, since women often make interior design decisions. Young and less affluent misses the mark, but Upcoming's data is shared with other sites.

Facebook	122.5 million/over 500 groups related to "interior design." Largest has 58,847 members. Few in Seattle, however.	Young (18-34), but more affluent. We could keep Facebook on the list, but perhaps not spend too much time on it until we test the results.
Yelp	25.7 million with 75 other interior design professionals in Seattle area. Only one had ratings; my client was listed, but hadn't claimed her page, and no reviews or ratings.	Female, young and less affluent, but highly educated. The less affluent bothers me a bit, but it couldn't hurt to try to get happy clients to post reviews. Search engines would pick up the data.
Twitter	23 million, but only people following will see posts, unless found through search.	Once again, female, young and less affluent for now. The growth rate is phenomenal and may prove useful as time goes on.
Slideshare	Nearly 1.2 million Searching for "interior design seattle," I found 227 slideshows.	No data at Quantcast
Dwell	68,861	Male, middle-aged, more affluent, educated. Jackpot!
Decorati	13,318	Female, middle-aged, more affluent, highly educated. I'm wondering if this includes interior designers, not customers?
Seattle Homes & Lifestyles Magazine	3,187	Female, middle-aged, more affluent, highly educated.

Once at Decorati, I took a look at the menu in search of Site Swag. Of course, I could advertise. Decorati Connect allows consumers to find a designer (an Angie's List of decorators you might say). But I needed to be a registered member to be a recommended designer. No problem, registration was free. And designers can add their portfolios and press links, too. Then there was the "Find a Designer" link. I also found forums and events under Community, where my client could easily respond to forum questions. Although I couldn't track down an easy way to add an event, I could send them an email request. The site even offers some handy advice to help designers market themselves through the site.

So here's what I came up with for a recommended short list, in priority order:

- Upcoming: this is first, since advance notice is needed for events.
- Dwell: get involved fully.
- Seattle Homes & Lifestyles: not a big audience, but it's local and targeted.
- Decorati: test it out.
- Facebook: join biggest decorating and travel groups.
- Yelp: take ownership of your page and get customers to write reviews.
- Slideshare: post portfolio here, so it's easy to add it to other social sites, email and at my client's website.
- Twitter: announce events, awards and published articles; add a Twitter link to the website and other properties to grow the list of followers.

Site Selection Checklist

- Look for sites that leverage your strengths.

- Match your target profile by geography, interest, demographic, activity and/or affinity. If meeting people face-to-face is important, look for sites that also host live events.

- Measure the amount of traffic they receive.

- Make sure the style and substance is a good fit.

- Review the site's media kit for more information about their visitors (if the site takes advertising, a link to it is usually found in the footer).

- Check out the blog, Q&A, groups or whatever you find there to see how active they are. You may also look to see how many new members have joined recently.

- If they pass muster, add them to your short list.

- Look for Site Swag promotional opportunities.

- Track your results and revise as necessary.

Try It Now

Now it's your turn. Make a list of the types of sites most appropriate for your business based on your marketing objectives and skills.

1. Start by choosing the right mainstream sites.

2. Create a general list of niche sites you think may be appropriate based on subject matter, geography and a general idea of target audience.

3. Narrow down your list to about 5 niche sites based on your research into audience composition and site traffic.

4. On those sites, make a list of the promotional freebies available (Site Swag). Create a chart listing the sites down the left side of the page. Across the top, list the types of Site Swag. Add checkboxes in the appropriate spots.

Chapter 15: Promotional Activities

This chapter is all about how to participate in the various types of social sites. There are more ideas and ways to use them than I can possibly list here, but it's a good start.

Blogs

Blogs are fairly simple to set up with tools like Blogger, WordPress and TypePad, and they're great for keeping your website content fresh (good for attracting search engines as well as return visitors). Writing skill and time is all it takes to keep up with a blog. You need to provide information that's relevant and of interest to your audience: give advice, let the reader in on a new discovery, relate an idea, etc.

There are many ways to take advantage of blogs. Sometimes they're used in place of a company website, especially when it's for some type of consulting. The idea is that people will be drawn to the advice and news, and then will go deeper into the site to learn about the services offered. Blogs are often used by startups, or any other type of business that wants to keep people informed about new developments. They're useful for customer support, providing a simple way to communicate service changes and sales promotions.

There's no point in having a blog if you have no readers. Here are some ideas for increasing your audience:

*   Write information of interest to your audience and put it in digestible formats, like lists. See Chapter 23 for more ideas.

- Include linkbait. It's great content in your blog that people will want to link to – think charts, checklists, unique images, links, etc. Tag your posts with keywords.

- Put a link to your blog in all your properties.

- At your blog, add the RSS icon so people can subscribe.

- Save your own blog at bookmarking sites, and remind readers to bookmark the posts in your blog entries.

- Add tools like AddThis to make it easy for readers share your information.

- Use Twitter and TwitterFeed to connect your network with your blog entries.

- Hint at the content of your blog entries on forums and discussion lists.

- At social sites you belong to, use applications that pull your blog onto your pages, like LinkedIn's BlogLink.

- At the sites where you're sharing your blog, make sure they're set up to ping you, so they're automatically notified about updates. Use a tool like Ping.fm to set up the notifications.

- Highlight your posts on a Squidoo lens.

- Search "increase your blog readership" to find even more ideas than I've listed here.

Blog Not Required

People are hearing so much about blogs that they think it's essential to have one of their own. That's not true. It takes a lot of time and energy to maintain a blog, let alone get people to read it. These days, people run blogs as a business. If writing isn't your forte, you may want to skip the blog or at least focus more time on other promotional opportunities.

Whether you write your own or not depends on a number of factors. If your main objective is to drive website traffic, it may be easier to leverage another site's blog traffic – find the ones of interest to your target audience. Connect with influential people in your community or industry. Look for thought leaders by finding the source of an interesting story or the ones who have a lot of followers. Hitch your wagon to their star by making valuable contributions to their posts, but don't just tag along. Say something useful or interesting – add value. However, be careful about what you write. Blogs are often monitored and the website owner will review the entries and determine which ones they allow. They do this to keep spammers from polluting their sites and diluting the value of their content. Don't try to spam or be too self-promotional. That just makes you look like an opportunist, and even if you are, you don't want to come across that way. On the other hand, you'll want to monitor comments on your blog, too.

Once you comment, your name will link back to the website or blog you provided when you signed up on the site. If the site doesn't work that way, try putting your link in the posting.

I was on a site called Aweber, which is an automated email tool. They had a blog entry in their *Inbox Ideas* that mentioned how to time marketing emails. I just happened to have written a blog entry on this topic. Now granted, in this case I had my own blog, but it could easily have been a link to a Web page or an article. I made a comment in the Aweber comment area that read, "I've got more information on this topic in my blog, and the entry is called 'Get a Life (cycle)'." It was in answer to the question, "How often should I send email to my customers?" And I provided a link. It drove a lot of traffic; not just any traffic. It included people who were interested in the specific topic. However, not every blog is going to allow you to do this. I got cyber-slapped once, because the social network I was on said I wasn't allowed to link back to my site.

Trackbacks

A better way to manage this is with trackbacks, which are links provided by a website publisher that allow you to link what you've written about them to their original post. Here's how it works:

1. Reference an article in your blog post, and include a link to the original article in the form of a URL or permalink.
2. Copy the trackback link from the original post's site (this is different than the link referenced above).
3. Add this link to your blog's trackback page or add it to the place that says something like "URL's to ping." If your blogging tool doesn't let you do this, try the tool from Simpletracks. This will let the original site know you've referenced their article. Whew.
4. It's up to the original site to accept your trackback. Once that happens, a link to your entry will appear in that blog's list of trackback "pings." That in turn may encourage their visitors to come to your site.

After all this, the original author still may not approve your trackback, which means you could go back to my original idea of commenting on their site and adding a link to your site (and deal with the consequences).

Microblogs

In my mind, microblogs like Twitter are best used for research, project management, sales promotions and sales support. I wouldn't say it's the best for building awareness or communicating a lot about a company. For research, it's an easy way to track people of interest, find connections and get clued into the latest industry news. Use a microblog to announce events, blog posts and other basic communications. If sales promotions are part of your promotional mix, they're great for posting coupons, discounts and sales. Set up your own microblog with Yammer to manage a team project in your company.

Microblogs are also ideal for time-sensitive information, so use it in situations where immediacy is important. For example, reporters are always looking for timely information. If you're trying to get some press, find the reporters that cover your industry. Start by choosing to follow the appropriate publications. If it's small, the publication itself may have a Twitter account. If it's big, individual journalists or editors may have accounts. You can also type the name of the publication into the Twitter search tool, or try typing in the word "magazine" for a list. You can also find lists of journalists by searching "Twitter journalists" in a search engine. When posting, use keywords to help them find you. Better yet, try following them to see if they'll follow you back. Hopefully, you've written content that they're interested in. Once they're following, you can send them direct messages (which can only be read by the person you send it to) about a news item or story idea.

Microblogs are also useful for immediate communications and alerts, good for letting people know about perishable inventory, such as tickets, hotel rooms, seats, tables, etc.

The real benefit of Twitter is the ease of use with which it can be used for mobile communications. Once someone opts into the mobile feature, Tweets are delivered as text messages (text is standard on mobile phones, so the recipient doesn't need an iPhone or Blackberry to get them). The most useful information when someone is mobile are items like flight delays, location changes or meeting times. Or they could be hanging out on Twitter for fun, to keep in touch with friends or to kill time.

The value of microblogs rests on the number of people who are following a Twitter account, because for the most part, they're the only ones who see the messages. A huge following is required to match the reach of other media (unless the information is so exciting that it spreads virally like wildfire through the Internet).

Some people get a tremendous number of followers just by following a lot of people. That happens because some people automatically follow anyone who's following them. It's indiscriminate – a numbers game – rather than having any defined purpose or rationale. Unless you're trying to get as many followers as you can, be selective about who you follow. Following too many people with too many posts, makes it difficult to sort through the junk. You'll end up slogging through a lot of useless blather. There are some people who post incessantly about what they had for breakfast and what their kids are doing at school. If you're interested on a personal level that's one thing, but if you want business information, you may not want to follow those people.

Plus, when there are so many posts, the information is fleeting because they pop up in chronological order. Posts quickly disappear among all the other ones that appear seconds afterwards (which of course depends on the number of people the viewer is following and how often they post). That means your message doesn't last long either.

Some people say this type of communication can build relationships. I'm not so sure. Keeping up connections via 140-character posts (separated by dozens if not hundreds of other posts) is even harder than keeping a relationship going in email (although you can use "GET [username]" to read all the posts of one person to capture a thread).

More microblog tips:

- Read the directions at the microblog you've signed up for and get familiar with the shortcuts, like using the @ in front of your user name so people follow you. Twitter has added a "101" guide for business; you'll find a link to it in the footer of their pages.
- Create interesting posts. Pose questions. Pass along breaking news. If your information is good, people will pass it on. On Twitter, this is known as a "retweet."
- Consider the difference between a post that's seen by everyone and a direct message to a specific person – it's kind of like the

difference between "reply" and "reply all" in email. However, you can only direct message someone who is following you.

- Add a link on the contact page of your website to make it easy to create a Twitter direct message. You could say, "Send me a direct message on Twitter" with the link: http://twitter.com/direct_messages/create/robbinblock (use your Twitter name in place of mine).
- Respond in a timely way to people mentioning your company, i.e., with @yourcompany or to those who send you direct messages.
- Announce blog or website updates. Provide a headline, paraphrase the interesting part and add a link. To keep your posts within the character limit, use TinyURL or Bit.ly to create short hyperlinks. Bit.ly also provides stats on the number of clicks your link received.
- Keep in touch with current contacts to reinforce existing relationships. It's the easiest and fastest way to communicate, so people are more likely to use it.
- Choose to follow groups, companies or associations of interest. Look for "follow me" links at their websites.
- Organize followers and posts by creating lists on specific topics.
- Follow your favorite authors (I choose ones related to small business, marketing, etc.), journalists and bloggers to keep up with industry news and ideas.

…and here are some Twitter applications you may want to try (there are literally hundreds):

- Use Listorious to find and promote your lists.
- Use SocialOomph if you want to set up Tweets now to appear later.
- Add something like Twitterfox to your Firefox browser to receive notifications about when people in your network Tweet.
- Find new contacts. Use Twitter's search to find people interested in similar subjects. Try following them to see if they'll follow you back.

- Once you find them, try TweetCloud to see if you're interested in the topics they're talking about.
- Find more tools at Wired's Wiki, Mashable or Twittgroups.

Get people to follow you

Posting on microblogs makes more sense if you have the right followers. Just like a website or blog, it needs to be promoted. Start with the following:

- Sign up to the microblog with the name you're known for, whether that's your real name, company name, or something else, so it's easier to find you when people do a search.
- Invite people to follow you.
- Add a "follow me" link on your website and on other properties and communications.
- When you're notified that people are following you, you may choose to follow them in return; then their followers have a chance to find you.
- Post frequently, but don't post so often that you turn people off and they stop following you.

If I were to summarize the industry pundits on what results in a lot of Twitter followers, here's a list in order of most followers to least:

1. Being known or famous, like an actor, model, spokesperson, author or beloved brand. Quoting Doshdosh, "They used their websites or platforms to promote their Twitter profile."[65]
2. Have a media entity, i.e., well-read blog, radio program, TV show, book, newspaper column, popular website, etc.
3. Make announcements about popular content, including links to other people's information. If you write articles or have a blog, share it on Twitter by adding the link:

http://twitter.com/home?status=[text you want to appear; use "+" for spaces; and the actual link to the article]. For example, the link to my article on xxxx would be: http://twitter.com/home?status=xxx+xxx+http://tinyurl.xxx.

4. Follow others, because people follow-back, even without thinking about it. I've seen people who don't post, but have a lot of followers, which means they're following in a knee-jerk fashion. If this is useful to you, go right ahead.

5. Promote their Twitter address. Just like marketing anything else, think about the people you want to attract and the type of content that would interest them. Then publicize your Twitter account by posting your address everywhere you'd put your website address: business card, website, blog, email signature, etc.[66]

Social Networks

Social networks are great for building community, keeping in touch with contacts, meeting new people through affinity groups and so much more. As discussed, you'll want to pick the right ones to participate in, because you can't do them all. Here are some ideas for making the most of a social network:

- Before jumping in with both feet, check to make sure the site is appropriate for your business. Look for Site Swag discussed in Chapter 14.
- If it meets your objectives and matches your target audience, sign up and create a basic profile.
- Set your privacy and email notification settings.
- When you have time, go back and complete your profile. Customize your pages. Then start posting content and participating. Add people to your network, join groups, vote, comment, answer questions, etc.
- Look around the site for buttons, links, widgets or badges to add to your properties.

- Look for ways to automatically share your content, either by pulling it into the site or by sharing it from the social network.

LinkedIn Company Profiles

B2B social networking site LinkedIn is known for its professional listings and offers the ability to view Company Profiles. According to their blog, you can "see over 160,000 profiles of companies on LinkedIn, ranging from Fortune 500 companies (e.g. eBay) to philanthropic organizations (e.g. Bill & Melinda Gates Foundation) as well as LinkedIn's own Company Profile page."[67] You can even create your own company profile, no matter how small your company.

The information is useful, whether you're researching an industry, writing a business plan, or trying to find sales leads by company. It could also help you get some exposure for your own company. According to LinkedIn's blog, data is aggregated from their database and combined with basic industry information from *Business Week*. Company Profile include:

- Number of people in your network who work at that company
- New hires, recent promotions and changes
- Most popular profiles
- Individuals in the news
- Related companies
- Key statistics: location, industry, type, company size, revenue, year founded, web address and employee stats

Facebook Pages

Facebook is such a dominant force that I couldn't go without explaining their pages feature – sometimes referred to as "fan pages." Unlike personal pages which are only viewable by friends, they're available for anyone to see. They may be found through the site's search or the advertising link at the bottom of any screen. Pages were designed by the company to be used for celebrities, bands and businesses. According to Facebook, "Fans of your Page won't be able to see that you are the Page admin or have any access to your personal account."

Fan pages can include general content, updates and events, among other things. You can even add applications. Gydget, for example, provides a way to update band fans about events. Just be aware that not all applications available for a personal page can be added to these pages.

Fan pages are easy to set up, but just like any property, they need to be promoted to gain a following – connect the page with appropriate groups, other social sites, create a badge, add the page's link to properties and communicate regularly with fans.

You should also know that if you're not interested in setting up a personal profile, Facebook allows you to create a Business Account. It offers limited access, but it's an option if you'd rather put a fan page up without creating a personal account.

Social Content Sites

Content sites feature news, articles, videos, podcasts, slideshows, images, games, widgets or any combination thereof. If you have the time, talent and inclination to create content, you're already different than the majority of people participating in social media and you have the potential to derive more benefit from it. Good, original material has more impact overall, because it has a greater potential of being shared, which is more potent than simply being the one doing the sharing.

Now that's not to say you can't place content elsewhere, like on your website and other types of social sites, but content sites like YouTube, Flickr and SlideShare have additional functionality that allow you to do some pretty cool stuff.

Many content sites allow you to embed the site's content into your website. This is done by copying and pasting the HTML code of the item into your website. With YouTube, for example, you can find videos of interest to your audience to build engagement and keep your site fresh – even if you don't have videos of your own. You can also create your own channel there. I often pick up materials created by CommonCraft and post them to my blog. Sure, people can search YouTube themselves, but you're adding value by filtering thousands of videos to find the appropriate ones for your audience. Write a helpful introduction to add even more value.

On Flickr, you can do so much more than store and share your photos. You can create a profile, join or create a group of your own and add widgets to your website or other social sites. You can set limitations on who may view and use your images and invite people to place your photos on their site. Be sure to ask for a photo credit, especially if you're a professional photographer. If you're hosting an event, use event photos to promote future events. You can tie Upcoming to Flickr (they're both owned by Yahoo), post photos to blogs, and save photos to your favorites and then share them.

Use SlideShare's event functionality to promote, archive presentations and documents, and to send out invitations. They'll list your event on their homepage and create a direct link to a signup page. You'll need to email them to get this set up though.

There are also tools like Yahoo Pipes and Squidoo that allow you to create social content sites of your own by combining feeds from other sources to create unique pages and applications.

Here are some ideas for making the most of the content you provide:

- Take creative risks to grab attention and people will be more likely to look at what else you've published. Stand out by being different. Use images no one else would use; try associating odd content with what you do; crop images differently. At least be more creative than your competition. Avoid clichés. But don't try to grab attention for the sake of grabbing attention. Think about what will excite your audience in particular.

- Share content in a timely way. If you just hosted or attended an event, get it online as soon as possible. People have short memories – they'll be on to the next thing quickly. The closer to your event you can get your photos up, the more likely people will share it with others, which in turn can drive traffic to your site. For more ideas about timing, see Chapter 17.

- Create collections of images, and select an attention-getting thumbnail to promote the entire album. The thumbnail by default is usually the first image in the collection. Make sure you change it to the one that offers the most compelling reason to see the rest of the set. Often, the content site will provide a link to your collection(s), which you can add to your properties or give to people to share.

- Actively promote and approve reuse of your content to help spread the word about you and your business.

- Maintain your online presence by updating the information on all your properties to keep the momentum going.

Shopping & Review Sites

There are hundreds of shopping and review sites, and in some cases, people who are looking for specific products and services are going to these first before using a search engine.

The first item on your agenda is to go to the appropriate sites to see if you're listed there. If you offer a service locally, start with Yelp. If you offer a travel service or destination, take a look at TripAdvisor. If you're an instructor, try Teachstreet. For clothing, try StyleHive. For handmade goods, there's Etsy. For books, go to Amazon. If you're already listed, be sure to claim ownership of it if you can. If you're not, add your site. Make sure the profile information the site has about you is accurate. On Yelp, go to the "Business Owners" link in the footer for more options.

The more reviews you get, typically, the higher your listing on these sites. You'll want to encourage positive reviews and manage negative ones (we'll talk about how to keep track of them in Chapter 18).

To encourage reviews, ask your best customers, and add requests on your website, in your newsletter and at your place of business. Don't write fake ones. Add links to your business cards and other properties. Ask for a review right after the person has purchased, attended an event, etc. If you get a few that aren't stellar, don't worry. That gives other reviews more credibility, because no one believes perfection exists (unless of course you're a Virgo like me). But be aware that some studies have shown that 90% of shoppers avoid shopping at *online* sites with bad reviews.[68] Check out Yelp for a good list about getting reviews; they just as easily apply to other review sites, as well.

Give your fans ideas for what to say, but make it unbiased so they express their own opinions. Reviews should be authentic and not sound cookie-cutter. Here's an example of a message I've used:

I hope you've enjoyed my classes as much as I have enjoyed teaching them. I'd appreciate it if you would share your comments with others who may be interested in taking a class.

Please take a moment to visit my profile on TeachStreet and write a quick review. Here are some ideas, but feel free to write whatever you like:

What you learned
What you liked or didn't (heaven forbid!)
The one great idea you walked away with
The best or worst of the whole thing
Whether or not you would attend another in the future

Thanks mucho

You may also want to incorporate the reviews you get into your website. They may just provide enough incentive to turn tire-kickers into actual buyers. Some review sites even provide links to make that connection easy.

If you get a negative review, consider the source. Think about how seriously others may take the comments and the damage they might cause. You'll need to determine if it's something you need to address or if you can let it go. If it's something you feel should be addressed, think about how you can turn the situation around. Once you've thought about what you might say, such as explaining why the reviewer may have received bad service, decide if it makes sense to post a public comment for all to see or to contact the person directly to correct the problem first. In either case, don't get defensive. If you go with the latter and it has a positive outcome, encourage them to add to their original post. People will have a more favorable view if you can resolve an issue, even if it started out badly. Some sites are now building in tools for addressing negative reviews, as well (see Chapter 20 for more on this topic).

If you're thinking about paying for an enhanced listing, which some sites offer, hold off on that until you spend more time getting your fans to write reviews. Check your traffic stats. If you find people are getting to you from that site, then you'll know your target audience is using it. It then might make sense to pay for the enhanced listing to drive even more traffic. The next chapter goes into more detail about when it makes sense to pay.

Bookmarking Sites

Being tagged or saved at a bookmarking site can increase awareness of your business and drive traffic to your website.

Here are a few ways you can use bookmarking sites for promotions:

- Start by bookmarking your own website.
- Put keywords and tags in your description.
- Bookmark your social content, articles you've written, and other sites related to your expertise and business.

Startups may want to establish profiles on key social sites somewhere between the time they register their domains and when they're ready for launch.

- Subscribe to recent bookmarks that others have saved on topics you're interested in to create an updated list of interesting bookmarks.
- Make friends with people who are bookmarking related sites.
- Just like other social sites, the more you engage, post, comment or whatever, the more people are likely to see your information.
- Use the Firefox plug-in Socialmarker to find and submit to appropriate bookmarking sites.
- Make it easy for people to bookmark your pages by adding links to your properties.

Social Calendars

If you host events, speak publicly, manage trade shows or work for a venue, this section is for you. Online calendars are an inexpensive way to publicize events – you make the announcement and the social components help you spread the word. I've mentioned Yahoo's Upcoming, but there are dozens of online calendars. Another is MatchboxCalendar that makes it easy to share an individual's events.

It's difficult to find the time to post on all of them, so be selective about the ones you use:

- Pick sites that are appropriate for your type of event and audience. For example, Upcoming has a lot of geek events, Teachstreet lists classes and workshops and Eventful is for music and arts lovers.

- Check your website stats to see which calendars are sending the most traffic and list on these first. Figure out where else your traffic is coming from, and visit these sites to see if they let you post events.
- Use sites that share posts with other sites: Upcoming, Eventful, Technorati, Ping-o-matic, Delicious and Google Calendar. Zvents shares with some major newspaper sites.
- Look for local sites that have their own calendars, like newspapers, industry associations, organizations and chambers of commerce. Keep in mind how the type of event and the distance people need to travel will influence attendance to determine how local the site needs to be. Granted, these sites may not be social per se, but you can't overlook them if you do events.
- Some sites offer extra features you may find useful. For example, TeachStreet automates a Craigslist posting for you.
- Beyond the calendar sites, many other types of sites allow you to post events, such as LinkedIn. Facebook's news feed shares events with your network automatically. When they sign up for the event, it prompts their friends to do so, as well. Slideshare allows you to create an event, invite registrations and save presentations. At their editorial discretion, they may even feature your slide deck on the homepage.
- Select a hashtag (described on page 177) to represent the event, business name or brand. Make it short and sweet. Remind attendees to use it on all your properties. Add a widget that tracks the hashtag on your website or blog. Create one with a tool like Tweetgrid.
- Invite friends to the calendar sites where you've posted events. Add an invite link to your website, or more specifically, your events page if you have one.
- Add badges or widgets from the calendar sites to your properties., like Eventful's countdown-to-the-day widget to encourage visitors to sign up sooner than later.

Wikis

Wiki's can be used for both managing and promoting your business, because they provide an easy way to collaborate and share information. You can either participate in an existing Wiki or create one of your own. The key difference between a Wiki and a social site is that much of the content, not just the comments, wall, etc. of a social networking site, are open to change by anyone given permission to do so.

A Wiki can help you support your marketing operations, aligning the people, processes and materials you need to execute your marketing plans. You can communicate with all the people on a project or in your business, and it can help you keep track of all the information in one place. As a place for links and files, you can store and keep track of market research, useful resources, process documents, new product ideas, useful lists and pretty much anything you can think of that needs to be shared among a group of people. They can also be useful for providing information to clients or simply brainstorming on a project. I've even seen them used to organize events, where people can add their names to a guest list.

Wiki's can be used to extend your Internet presence. For example, articles featured on well-trafficked Wikipedia and wikiHow can provide a lot of exposure because they rank very high in search engines. But don't dismiss the niched sites, like Wikicompany and Wikitravel, where it may be easier to get your information listed.

Tools like Wetpaint or Wikia (by Jimmy Wales, the creator of Wikipedia) allow you to create your own Wikis. They can be public or private Wikis, so you decide who's allowed to view and participate.

Wikis can be an easy way to add fresh content to your site without having to do all the work yourself, like you would if you were to write your own blog. You could create a place where you post glossaries, helpful lists and resources, and then other people can add their contributions. Once it's created, simply link your site to it or embed it in your site.

To encourage collaboration and keep fresh contributions coming in, you'll need to promote your Wiki and invite people to it. Remember to let go of your promotional brain if you're trying to create an open community, and focus on encouraging dialog and other types of contributions by users.

Whether you're on someone else's Wiki or your own, monitor your entries regularly to make sure the information is correct and up to date.

Email

Although there's been speculation that social media will replace email, I beg to differ. Communicating directly to your list via email has a much different effect than say, people following you on Twitter. The difference is that social media is passive – people have to seek it out. Email is pushed to the inboxes of people who've elected to receive the information. That's not to say there aren't delivery issues with email; getting bumped by spam filters is one of them. But if you ask people to add you to their address book, that risk is reduced.

Cannibalization is something to consider, as well. Some people would rather communicate via their social networks, rather than choose to receive email directly. That means you need to take advantage of the email tools available on these sites. Others are signing up for RSS feeds in an attempt to de-clutter their email inboxes. However, you may choose to offer exclusive information in the the emails you send, which means they run the risk of missing out if they only get their information via a feed. It's up to you to decide how exclusive that email information is and letting people know that for the strategy to have an effect. The risk of cannibalization in this case may be small however, since as we've seen, many people aren't familiar with the benefits of RSS.

That being said, there are four areas where email and social media intersect:

Personal email Sometimes when you meet someone through social media, you want to continue the conversation off-network. Of course, you'll need their email address to do so. That isn't always available until one of you decides to provide it.

Another way to take advantage of personal email to fulfill a social objective is to add a signature to all your emails that includes links to your networks.

Narrowcast email Take the opportunity to grow your network connections by adding links or badges to your promotional emails and newsletters. Add sharing tools too, so people can distribute them to their social networks. ShareThis is working with an email marketing service to allow you to do just that. It's like "Forward to a Friend" on steroids.

The most effective mailing lists are those that you develop yourself, rather than the ones you purchase. You'll get a better response from people who opt-in to receive your mail versus strangers. You can leverage social networks to build your list, but you shouldn't be scraping a network's website for addresses. However, if you have the right content, you may be able to attract visitors to your website, where you can provide a way to sign up for your list.

When sending email, think about what makes your email relevant and valuable to the reader. It could be educational information, event announcements, sales promotions or whatever. If your content is interesting and useful, people will choose to stay on your list. If not, you risk losing the opportunity to communicate with them. The look and feel of your email is secondary to the list and content, but still important. It should be professional, well designed and visually branded. Your writing style can help keep people engaged, as well.

For distributing email use the available tools to make your life easier, rather than your desktop email program. They're fairly low cost, allow you to add images easily, are more likely to get past spam filters and they come with reporting tools so you can see who is reading your email. Some are starting to integrate social tools that make it easy to share your content, as well. Most of these are hosted solutions, which means you use them through a website and there's no software to download. Pricing is based on a monthly flat rate or by the number of contacts or emails sent per month.

Notifications When setting email options in a social network profile, be sure to opt-in to receive personal emails for conversations you've been following. This will allow you to keep up with ongoing conversations, so you can respond in a timely manner without having to revisit the place where you originally made a comment.

Archives When you join a group, there's usually a place where you can choose to receive periodic digests of the group's activities. There are two benefits to receiving these emails. One is that you can learn from what other members are doing and find new opportunities. The other is that your name will pop up if you've been active. It's just another way to get your name in front of the other members, without having to do anything in addition to the original activity. Of course, the only people who see them are those that have set their notifications as such, but it may help you get the attention of those who have.

Strategies and Tactics

The following chart provides a summary of strategies and social tactics we've discussed.

Social Activities and AIDA

Join social sites	Build enhanced profiles	Answer questions	Provide links to website, blog and RSS feed
Invite your contacts to your networks	Consistently comment with key messages	Create and upload original content	Add social site badges to your site
Find and research new contacts	Post events to online calendars	Voice an opinion	Use chiclets and widgets to cross-pollinate
Get listed on review sites	Offer controversial or provocative content	Share news, case studies, statistics...	Install sharing tools
Tag content with keywords			Use limited time offers, coupons, etc.
Vote, comment update...			

Participate in group discussions
Create your own group
Microblog, blog, vlog
Share social bookmarks

Chapter 16: When It Makes Sense to Pay

I usually recommend that small businesses exhaust all the appropriate ways to promote before they start spending money. It's a tradeoff. If you have more time than money, avoid spending. If you have more money than time, then it can make sense to pay.

You can get a lot of promotional bang for the buck from social sites, considering that there are so many things you can do for free. But there are times when it makes sense to pay for the services that keep the social sites in business. Many support themselves through a combination of premium services, ecommerce, licensing and advertising. Let's take a look at some of these, what they offer and when it makes sense to use them.

Premium Services

Depending on the type of site, premium services can include access to in-depth research data, the ability to contact people outside your network, pro-level functionality, and more. The decision to pay depends once again on what you're trying to accomplish.

Here are just a few examples:

One of the best deals on the Net is an upgraded account from Flickr that includes unlimited uploads and storage, account stats, ad-free browsing and sharing, and high-definition video uploads/playback. LinkedIn provides access to people outside your network, which means you can send messages without being introduced first or receive leads on a weekly basis based on your own search criteria. LinkedIn also allows market researchers to survey their members.

Sometimes paid memberships provide greater visibility in directories, and possibly higher search engine rankings, with featured listings at the top of a page or placement in several categories (in essence a form of advertising). This could be useful when lists are undifferentiated and the reader only views the first part. Some sites also allow you to customize and therefore differentiate your profile with logos or multimedia.

Advertising

Many social sites offer brand and performance-based advertising opportunities. In general, there are two formats. Display ads, which are image-based banners, are for brand advertising. They come in many shapes and sizes, which have been standardized by the Internet Advertising Bureau. Advertisers pay for these in advance and by impressions – the number of times an ad will be seen on a Web page. The price is based on the number of visitors the site attracts. A common measurement is CPM or Cost Per Thousand. For every 1,000 impressions (the number of times your ad is seen on a page), it will cost $X. This allows you to make an apples-to-apples comparison among different websites.

Text-based ads are typical of performance advertising, which are also known as Pay-Per-Click (PPC are like the Google ads you see down the right side of a search results page) or Pay-Per-Performance (PPP). The performance part varies. Sometimes a site is paid when someone simply clicks on an ad; sometimes an actual purchase has to be made.

For mainstream sites that attract large numbers, display ads are typically out of budget range for the small business. If you think banner advertising is something you'd like to test, try a niche site with fewer, but more targeted, viewers. It will be cheaper than advertising on a big site. Text ads, on the other hand, are more approachable. For example, Facebook offers PPC advertising starting at a minimum of $1/day. LinkedIn recommends their text advertising program for companies with budgets under $25,000.

Behavioral Targeting

Typically, ads displayed on websites are placed contextually based on the content of the website page. On social sites, ad placement is behavioral. In other words, ads are placed based on the profile information or web surfing patterns of website visitors. Social sites are basically taking advantage of the user profile data that people readily volunteer and advertisers need, like age, gender and location. On Facebook and MySpace, marketers don't buy ads tied to search terms. Instead, the ads are linked to information that users reveal about themselves on the sites, such as their age, hobbies or other personal interests.[69] The data may also be combined with prior transactions to target even further.

A big issue with behavioral targeting is that it's considered an invasion of privacy by some, because a cookie or unique identifier may be used to track the websites someone visits or their behaviors at those sites. This data is used to determine the content and advertising the site will serve. It is believed that ads targeted this precisely will be more relevant to the visitor than those placed randomly or contextually, resulting in increased conversions or sales. Some social media sites have run into violation of privacy issues with this technique.[70]

Effectiveness

Advertising effectiveness in general rests on several factors including the industry, website content, reach, target and creative ad content. It can also depend on how the ad is delivered in relation to the people someone knows. Marketers "are finding that if our friends buy something, there's a better-than-average chance we'll buy it too."[71]

However, advertising to date on certain types of social sites hasn't been very effective. "For all its popularity, Facebook has yet to prove itself as an advertising platform. Visitors, it seems, focus on their friends and pay scant attention to ads."[72] It's not that surprising, considering most people trust a referral from a friend, rather than information in an advertisement. This seems especially true today, as more people are overwhelmed and skeptical about the marketing messages they're bombarded with every day. A comScore study found that 28% of respondents were likely to notice advertising on social media, but only 23% of those are likely to trust them. That puts social advertising behind other media, like TV, newspapers and corporate websites. Some industries, like entertainment, get better results.[73] That makes sense, since entertainment is a natural fit in a social setting. The ads can also be more exciting and interactive.

Jupiter Research suggests that advertisers may want to stick with blogs, which weigh heavier in purchase decisions than social networks:

25% of blog readers say they trust ads on a blog.

19% trust ads on social networking sites.

40% of blog readers have taken action as a result of viewing an ad; of those, 16% have sought more information on a product or service and 16% have visited a manufacturer or retailer Web site.[74]

Sponsors of the survey say blogs offer more specific and personal information from an authority on a specific niche topic. Valerie Combs, VP of Corporate Communications at BuzzLogic, believes it "…creates a level of trust with the reader… ."[75]

In addition, a Chicago Tribune article noted "…starting a conversation with consumers also can be more effective than placing ads on social networking sites. A recent survey by research firm IDC shows that even though more than half of U.S. consumers with Internet access are on social networking sites, only 57 percent of those users clicked on at least one ad in the past year versus 79 percent of overall Web users."[76]

Just like any other medium, advertising seems to be a necessary evil for keeping social networks alive, but it could have a negative impact on the use of those social networks. "Annoyed with the ad deluge on social networks, many users are spending less time on the sites."[77]

Considering that the mainstream sites are having a tough go of it, you'd think the niche sites with smaller audiences would have more difficulty convincing marketers to advertise. However, very targeted sites like The Knot for brides-to-be, seem to be hosting a variety of advertisers. This could be because people are visiting the site for specific information and advice, and when someone sees a recommendation for where to buy a wedding dress – whether that's from a friend or they see it in an ad – it may just be something they follow up on. As mentioned previously, mainstream social sites seem to be for hanging out with friends and family, not a place for making purchases.

Members of social networking sites are open to offers and promotions as long as they are targeted to their interests:

58% of nearly 800 users of social networking sites say very few ads and offers on them match their specific interests and preferences.

Another 29% say none of them do.

56% polled said the quality of their online experience would be improved if social networking sites provided more targeted advertisements and offers tailored to their specific interests and preferences.[78]

In an attempt to improve ad relevance, advertisers keep trying different models. "Facebook's Social Ads concept attempts to improve the relevance of advertising by mining the connections between Facebook members."[79]

Decision Factors

Before you decide to advertise, make sure you're maximizing the free services first. If you have more time than money, take advantage of the Site Swag first.

Consider the immediacy of advertising. You get to choose when and where it will appear; PR and social media take longer to have an effect. On the other hand, advertising on social sites is obviously not going to have the same impact as advertising on other media, such as in a magazine or on TV, because it may hit fewer people and the format may not be as exciting.

Advertising can make sense when you see a lot of traffic coming from a social site where you've been participating, because that says it's already sending you people interested in your product or service. Advertising on those sites could help you get the attention of people outside of your network.

Then there are times when advertising works best in combination with other media. An offline print ad for a new restaurant may encourage someone to visit a review site, or possibly check in with a foodie blog to see what people are saying about it.

"…a new survey from the Retail Advertising and Marketing Association (RAMA) finds that traditional advertising – especially in magazines – plays a big role in directing those searches. The poll found that 47.2% of shoppers are most likely to start an online search after viewing a magazine ad, while 43.7% said reading an article was most likely to send them surfing. TV ads (42.8%) came next, followed by newspaper ads (42.3%)."[80]

Before selecting a site to advertise on, be sure to check their stats and media kit. The site will typically provide valuable information about how many people use the site and their demographics. For example, data from LinkedIn included the following:

• 35,000,000+ Professionals and growing by 1 million members per month

- 750,000+ Senior Executives
- Executives from all Fortune 500 companies
- 46% are Business Decision Makers
- Average Age: 41
- Household Income: $109,000
- Over 450 million page views per month
- Over 560,000 professionals visit the LinkedIn homepage on a typical day
- 42 page views per member per week

You should also do some research on average click-through rates (CTR's), which are one way to measure effectiveness. For example, Google CTR's can range anywhere from .5% to 30% (the numbers are all over the map and are highly dependent on many factors including keywords, bid amount, ad location and the content).

To place an ad, you can either go directly to a site or place ads through an ad network, like Offer Pal Media. They deliver advertisements to a range of social sites.

Creative

What you say in an ad can impact its effectiveness as much as where you place it. Think about a social site's environment. People are there for so many other distracting reasons that you've got to be creative and highly targeted if you're going to grab someone's attention.

Today, viewers are exposed to a greater number of messages in a given time than ever before. That clutter and noise is making people less receptive. Unless you can afford to run a lot of ads or create one that blows people away, your message could easily be bypassed.

Over the past couple of years at least, promoters have incorporated games into their ads in the hopes of attracting an audience. But even kids are getting sick of the little games on Facebook. Sending hugs and whatever are of little interest, and it's obvious to at least some users anyway that games are designed to sell them something.

Just like in the real world, it's not surprising that people respond more positively to sales promotions. According to a Prospectiv survey, consumers said the types of tailored ads and offers they would respond to are:

- One-off coupons and discount offers from the brands and products they buy (62%).

- E-newsletters featuring coupons, discounts, news and tips about favorite brands (24%).

- Invitations to join interactive email groups, online forums and social networks for sharing and communicating (14%).[81]

Mitigating the Cost of Advertising

In some cases, media advertising is the ideal way to promote a business, particularly when it's important to reach a mass audience. It also allows you total control over the message and delivery. However, production and placement costs often put it out of reach of the small business. There are several ways to overcome this problem.

The most obvious is to trade off sweat for money. In other words, public relations may be used to reach a lot of people without the out-of-pocket cost of advertising. The cost to place an ad is dependent on the print publication's circulation or the electronic media's (TV/radio) coverage area. For web or social site display ads, you're paying for eyeballs – the number of people who visit a site. The bigger that number is, the more expensive it is to place an ad.

By using highly targeted advertising vehicles, you can find the precise audience for your message, which makes your ad buy less costly and more efficient. This means there's little waste. In other words, rather than advertising in a local newspaper with a large circulation, a business can purchase banner ads on a specific website, neighborhood social network, or find an industry newsletter with a small, but targeted circulation to reach its market. If you had advertised in the newspaper, your money would have been wasted on circulation that has nothing to do with the people you're trying to reach.

Thanks to the Internet, media has evolved from traditional to digital, but new media isn't a perfect substitute for the more traditional channels. They don't always have the same reach or impact. However, for the small business that doesn't need to reach as many people, they can be just right.

Another way to skirt the cost is negotiation. Depending on the particular publication or station, and especially if you're a first-time advertiser, you can negotiate for better rates. Just like any negotiation, it's important to understand what the medium wants and what you have to offer so you can get the best deal.

Getting into the differences, the pros and cons of each medium, and how to purchase media are beyond the scope of this book. I'd recommend reading up on the subject and hiring a professional before jumping in – it's easy to make expensive mistakes.

Chapter 17: Strategic Timing

Just like other media, it's important to figure out how to be efficient and squeeze more value from it. Proper timing is just another way to take advantage of synergy – that is, by coordinating your efforts time-wise, you'll derive more impact from it.

You have a better chance of being successful with social media if you time it right. To do that, schedule your activities to coincide with your customer's behaviors, seasonal purchase patterns, your business calendar and marketing activities. A regular schedule of participation will also help you stay on top of your social media strategy.

Schedule with other Marketing Activities

Time your participation to coincide with other marketing that you're doing, like a trade show. It will give you something to talk about and your activity will be more closely tied to the action you expect from the reader – that is in this case to come see your booth at the show.

Customer's State of Mind

As mentioned previously, putting a communication in proximity to where a purchase is made makes for more effective communication. This is also true in terms of timing your communications to coincide with the customer's state of mind. You want to be there when they're in the mood to listen or to buy.

One way to do this is to time the delivery of your message with the moment a prospect starts thinking about making a purchase (usually set off by a trigger event), and then follow up with another one when you think they're just about ready to make the final decision. Trigger events happen when things change in someone's life (birthday, anniversary, graduation, etc.) or business (retirement, job move, budgeting cycles, etc.). External factors can be triggers too, like upturns or downturns in the economy, regulatory issues, etc. Key transaction data, like date of purchase, quantity purchased, purchase frequency, etc. will provide a clue about when someone is ready to make another purchase.

With some businesses, you can make an educated guess about when someone is likely to make a repeat purchase based on their last one. For example, if you sell ink cartridges, there's a good chance you're going to know when they're likely to run out. That's when you send the follow up email, and throw in a coupon kicker to make the sale. By timing communication appropriately, you can be top-of-mind just when they're ready to place an order (otherwise known as the ripest moment).

Business Cycles

Another way to time your activities is in accordance with the cycles of your business or industry. For example, participate more frequently in advance of the months you know you're going to be slow. Or conversely, slow down your communications in anticipation of being too busy to handle the work or the orders.

Seasonality

Consider seasonality, holidays and school schedules, with Christmas being the biggest one. Either you're the type of business that's super busy during November-December, or things come to a crashing halt. Plan accordingly to flatten out the highs and lows. Your messages should be "seasonal" too, in that they should relate to what customers are thinking about at these key times.

Be aware that social sites are susceptible to seasonality, as well. Sites appealing to a young audience experience spikes in usage during the summer and holidays.[82] At other times, the sites may be so cluttered with similar messages that yours may not a have a chance of getting through, so your efforts could be wasted – better to save your communications for when they may actually be read.

Competition

Consider what the competition is doing or what's happening in your industry. Time your activities to coincide with or counteract these.

Editorial Calendars

Go online to find out what a site plans to write about – they issue this information in editorial calendars (you'll find this type of information in the media kit or under "advertise" in the footer of the Web page). In fact, if your audience is reading those publications, it's likely the magazine will stimulate interest in a topic. Why not jump on board with your own information that relates to these ideas? It's your contribution, so you can make it relevant and interesting to your particular audience. One of my clients created a software game that teaches preschoolers how to read. Parenting magazine, which runs a monthly story on toys for kids, is a perfect place to position my client's stories for their readers.

Your Own Publishing Calendar

It might also be useful to create your own editorial calendar, so you can plan to contribute timely content. Include the when, where and topic. Select a time period, say the next six months and list the subjects you're going to write about each month in your blog. It could be tied to important events in your customers' lives or you could write an educational series around a particular topic. You could also do this in a weekly or quarterly format. This way, you can see consistency throughout and make sure you're communicating what you really want to talk about at the right time.

Set Periodic Reviews and Updates

Another way to look at timing is to put yourself on a daily, weekly or monthly schedule. This will ensure that you're creating contributions regularly, and it may also help you to stay organized. Sometimes it isn't possible to be so rigid, and it could be just as easy to respond immediately when something's on your mind than putting it off until a scheduled time period (kind of like how you might manage email). So you may also think about organizing your contributions ad hoc (on the fly), frequently, periodically (regular intervals) or occasionally (once in a while when you have nothing else to do – but when is that?).

The idea is to match the timing of your communications with what's happening on your social scene so you keep the conversation moving, and choose what fits with your work style. Depending on how active your network is, you can take things faster or slower. Consider the types of sites you participate in and how active they are. Also, how important it is to respond immediately versus what can wait for another time. Also rate the value of the contributor and how fast you should respond by how close they are to you and how influential they may be to the rest of the group.

The following will give you an idea of how you can organize your time:

Timing Participation	
Triggered	• Respond when you receive an email notification about your post (make sure you've opted in to receive these email notifications).
Ad Hoc	• Answer group questions or Q&A's.
	• Share info of interest with your networks: use sharing tools, bookmarks, add links to properties, etc.
	• On Twitter, review new followers and follow them if appropriate.
	• Invite new people to your networks as appropriate.
Frequently	• Check your blog for comments and respond.
	• Check Twitter for mentions of your username (@robbinblock), real name and business name, and respond as necessary.
	• Check reputation management services to see if you've been mentioned, and respond as necessary.
	• Monitor these blog sites: Technorati, IceRocket, Google Blog Search and AllTop.

Periodically
- Issue press releases.
- Check your stats, then review and revise your social media marketing strategy.
- Create new content and repurpose for several formats (more often than once a week could interfere with your work schedule and affect the quality of your posts).
- Look for new tools at the sites you participate in to help you share and cross-pollinate.

Try It Now

1. Pull out the short list of sites you created earlier. Add the promotional activities you're going to do under each one.

2. Take a look at the paid advertising or sponsorship opportunities offered at each site. Weigh that information against the no cost opportunities.

3. Create your marketing calendar. Start by making a list of all the major dates, holidays, milestones and marketing activities that affect both your customers and your business.

   Chart months across the top of a page – six months to a year should be sufficient (make it as granular as you like. If monthly is too detailed, do it by quarters. If too general, break it down by weeks or days. For this overview calendar, you don't need to break it down by day, dayparts, i.e., morning, afternoon, evening, or specific time. Although social media's impact can be immediate and time-sensitive, that level of precise timing would be more appropriate for a specific campaign like one that supports a trade show, product announcement or business launch).

   Next, note the categories down the left side of the page:

- Customer behavior: purchase cycle, life stage, change in social media usage habits, times when they're more likely to be using social media, i.e., students at school vs. summer break
- Business behavior: launch dates, key milestones, anniversaries, etc.
- Seasonality
- Holidays, or other special days
- Marketing activities and events (i.e., trade shows, ad campaigns, sales promotions, etc.)
- Time zones
- Tie in the appropriate social media activities

Part V: Tracking Results

Measuring Social Media's Value
Review, Analysis & Interpretation

Tracking the results of your marketing activities is part of any good plan. During the planning process, it's important to know ahead of time how you're going to measure results. Ask yourself, "How are we going to know if we've been successful?" You'll want to look at the impact on your business in general, and drill down to the results derived from social media specifically. You'll be looking for improvements in website visibility, engagement, reputation and actions taken by prospects or customers – whether that's a contact, website visit, foot traffic or purchase. That information will help you decide whether it makes sense to continue your participation at the same level or whether you should point your energies and resources elsewhere.

Chapter 18: Measuring Social Media's Value

For any business, a combination of micro and macro factors are what make it successful, so it isn't easy to tease out the effect that social media has on the bottom line. It's difficult to connect a social activity with a specific sale. However, we can look at sales trends and long-term changes in brand awareness, name recognition and reputation to see its impact. There are also indicators specific to social media activities that can be measured, like the number of interactions and comments, network growth and referral website traffic.

To take a reading of your business, start by tracking all the steps along the purchase cycle from the moment someone first hears about you through to that final sale. Look at actual numbers, such as:

- Inquiries by phone and email
- Foot and/or website traffic
- Coupon and coupon code redemption
- Sales transaction data (on and offline): who, what, when, where
- Individual purchase amount and frequency
- New customers or clients
- Sales revenue in units or hours, and dollars
- Profit margin and net profit

There are more ways to track than I care to count. However tempting it might be to look at every number, don't spend all your time playing with them. Establish your own performance standards. Make a list of what's important to your business and attach clearly defined objectives, like a percentage increase in website visits, number of coupons downloaded, increase in the number of followers, or newsletter signups to name a few.

Some of this information will come from your own business records. The next section talks about where to find the rest.

Web Analytics

The data coming off your website is one way to see the results of all your marketing efforts because many will respond by visiting your site. It allows you to see the affect you're having on your audience, what's driving traffic to your site, and how your visitors interact with your content.

The stats will also help you decide which social sites are best for promoting your business. It provides some level of "proof" about the sites that have sent you visitors. For example, I can tell from my website stats which online calendars are driving traffic. I then concentrate my energies on those sites, and perhaps drop the ones that aren't performing. I can always add them back to my list when I have more time.

Website analytics can answer the following questions:

- Am I getting more traffic to my website?
- Am I getting referrals from the social sites where I participate?
- What pages are people visiting as a result of my social networking?
- Is my site getting stickier? Are visitors staying longer, viewing more pages or are more people returning more frequently?
- What are the trends and what has changed?

In my consulting practice, building relationships with potential customers is what essentially gets me new leads. It starts with meeting people at my speaking engagements. From there, they visit my website. I surmise this from the *direct* traffic I see coming to my site, indicated by the 40.91% below. In other words, people get my Web address from my business card, and then when they're back at their offices, they visit my site. That is, people are going directly to my site by typing the URL.

All traffic sources sent a total of 3,992 visits

40.91% Direct Traffic

21.79% Referring Sites

37.27% Search Engines

Courtesy: Google Analytics

- Direct Traffic
  1,633.00 (40.91%)
- Search Engines
  1,488.00 (37.27%)
- Referring Sites
  870.00 (21.79%)
- Other
  1 (0.03%)

When someone finds you by typing words into a search engine and then land at your site, those results are called *organic.*

Now I don't know precisely how many people who visit my website actually come to the classes, because I don't manage the registrations. If I did, I would be able to connect the visitor to the actual attendance. I can surmise, however, that some of the people visiting my site are attending a workshop, signing up for a newsletter or helping me achieve another one of my goals.

The following is what I use to track results:

Goal	Measurement
Website traffic	• Website analytics
Event attendance	• Attendee count
Newsletter signups	• Email tool report

Requests to join my networks	• Emails received from social sites
Blog readership	• Website analytics (my blog is hosted in the same place as my website) • Number of comments • Number of subscribers • Blog Catalog and other tracking tools • Trackbacks
Article placement	• Number of inbound links • Search engine rank • SERP count
Connections	• Social site stats
Contacts or inquiries	• Number of emails • Number of phone calls • Invitations to networks

Analytics Tools

There are two ways to get your information. Almost every website host offers a way to see the information that's logged each time someone visits a website. These logs track the number of times a computer's browser makes a request to their computers (otherwise known as "servers"). A "request" is noted for each file (html, gif, jpg, wmv, etc.) sent to someone's browser.

If you're not tracking your website traffic, you're not alone. Almost half of the people in my classes don't know what website analytics are, let alone that there's usually a statistical tool included with their hosting package. Often, it's simply a matter of signing up for it online or contacting the host to turn it on.

The other type allows you to track page views directly. This includes services like the free Google Analytics. There are many others that provide more sophisticated information, but Google is a good, affordable start. Once you sign up, Google will provide you with a small bit of computer code to add to your site's template, so you can track each and every page. If you don't know how to do this, contact the person who set up your site or your webmaster. It's pretty easy to install and the reports can be easier to read than those from your host, depending on the tools they're using.

Specifically, look at the social sites visitors came from, how long they stayed and the pages they viewed. This will indicate what information they were interested in and what motivated them to visit your website. The numbers you're looking for include:

Unique visitors are the number of unduplicated individuals who visited your site. This gives you some indication of how many people know about you and how well your marketing is working overall.

Session Length shows how long a visitor stayed at a website. It's one way to measure stickiness (along with overall number of pages viewed, depth of visit and visitor loyalty). You might be able to interpolate that the longer they stayed, the more engaged they are.

Content refers to the pages the visitor viewed and offers an indication of interest and topics the visitor is interested in.

Navigation, Buy Flow or Process Flow indicates how visitors move around a site; particularly useful for ecommerce, because you can see what leads up to a sale (or where someone abandons or drops out of the flow).

Referrals indicate where your traffic came from, the path they took through your site, and where they went next. These behaviors may give you an idea of how they progress through the purchase cycle. The geographic data will show you the physical location.

The source of the referral can also be an indication of value. Organic results are more valuable, because the website visitor got to the site from a description based on a keyword match, rather than an ad. Conversion rates from organic are typically higher, too.[83]

Bounce Rate reveals tire kickers who don't stay long – they're only visiting one page, then leaving. Pages visited and session length indicate the ones who stay longer. Hopefully, they're reading more content. That means they're more engaged, and ultimately more qualified prospects.

Downloads Engagement can also be measured by the number of document downloads; videos viewed, podcasts streamed or coupons downloaded.

Visitor Loyalty is one indication of stickiness, because it shows how many people visit your site over and over again.

Special Website Pages

If you have specific campaigns you'd like to track, you might want to set up landing pages on your site. Rather than sending someone to your home page, you send them to a specific page with information related to that topic, query, offer or campaign. It's the digital equivalent of coupon codes or vanity phone numbers. Track the landing page of your site to determine how many people came from where, and then what they did next. This will help you figure out what they found interesting – or not – and if the campaign is working.

With each page, you may also set up forms or specific calls-to-action to measure the response to those. The number of responses divided by the number of visitors is the conversion rate. Google Analytics offers tools for tracking conversions, too.

Third Party Software Placed on Your Site

Third party software tools, particularly the web-based ones, offer some type of reporting. For example, narrowcast email providers, such as Constant Contact, Mail Chimp, RatePoint and Vertical Response to name a few, often provide a widget for collecting email addresses. Seeing the number of people who actually sign up for your mailing list is one way to measure engagement. They also provide email reports about open rates, bounces, click-throughs, forwards and more.

Widgets, like the ones from FriendFeed, Twitter and Blog Catalog, also offer data. Clicks on these by your website visitors indicate how much your information is appreciated.

Other Online Stats

Beyond tracking business data and website traffic, there are many other ways to measure progress. They include link popularity, search engine results and ranking, social site stats and reputation monitoring.

Link Popularity

It's good to know how many inbound links you have from other sites. Measuring them is easy to do using a tool like Yahoo's Site Explorer or WhoLinkstoMe. Search engines use link popularity to determine rank, as well.

Search Engine Results

When someone types keywords into a search engine, the results are ranked according to the site's formula or algorithm on the SERP (search engine results page). The closer the listing is to the top, the higher the rank.

Google rates the relative importance of websites based on a linking algorithm they call "PageRank." It assigns websites a number between 1 and 10 based on the number of credible inbound links Google identifies. The higher the PageRank, the more weight the site is given within search results. Many sites have a rank of "0." There aren't many with a PageRank of "10." To check your rank, use a tool like PRChecker.

Maintaining a high position can be costly, but a quick and inexpensive way to improve your odds is to sign up for Google Maps Local. When someone searches for a business with a location-related keyword, like a street, neighborhood or city near you, you're more likely to show up next to the map at the top of the results page.

You can also boost your position by making sure your site is optimized with the right keywords and by increasing your inbound links.

To see how you're doing on results pages, type your keywords into Google and some of the other search sites. Don't get this confused with typing in your name or business name; in that case, you're sure to show up on top, but that doesn't indicate your actual rank among all the possible results of a keyword search.

Another way to see how you're doing compared to other sites is to use Compete, Alexa or Quantcast. However, if you don't have significant traffic, you may not see much data.

Search Engine Watch offers a lot more information about SEO. But for now, we're focused on social media's contribution to rank, and that comes from getting links, mentions and conversations going at high traffic social sites.

Social Site Stats

Most social sites offer some kind of statistics about your activity and that of your network. Some are better at it than others. The numbers indicate level of interest and engagement. User ratings by stars, favorites, tag clouds and other folksonomies, although not scientific, can provide insight into engagement, reputation and image.

Your activity stats

- Invited 8 members
- 0 referrals given
- 1 referral received
- 1 Biz Talk post
- 10 Biz Talk comments
- 19 Article comments
- 13 events attended
- 2 events hosted
- 3 articles published
- 0 sponsorships given

Courtesy: Biznik

On Biznik, for example, you'll see the number of referrals, Biztalk comments, and profile views, which shows how others are responding to a member's social activity. Facebook offers the number of thumbs up/down and number of comments. They also offer something called Lexicon, which lets you find out what people are saying on the site. LinkedIn offers a "Who's viewed my profile", "Company Buzz" and a whole host of other stats beyond the activity stats shown at left.

The actual number of conversations going on has a certain value as well, "…the raw number of reviews or comments, and the proportion of positive and negative ones, send useful signals to other people, even if they do not trawl through all of them."[84]

Here are other numbers to look for:

- Invitations received/accepted.
- Followers, fans, group members or people joining your network (apart from ones you invited).
- Subscribers (email list, blog, RSS feed, newsletter).
- Comments received; interactions with your comments.
- Number of times your name, brand name, products, blog name, etc. appears.
- Content viewed, listened to, read, voted on, bookmarked, forwarded, downloaded, embedded, tagged, shared, etc.
- Other data may include responses to on-site surveys, polls or Q&A's.

Also take a look at the information being shared by popularity and staying power. Is it being shared and retrieved on the same day or does it have a long shelf-life, continuing to be retrieved over a long period of time? Bit.ly, ShareThis and AddThis are some of the tools that help you track that type of information.

Reputation Monitoring

As we've said, there's more to tracking than hard numbers. They mean something of course, but what people are actually saying – about you, your company, your products and services in comments and conversations can be valuable feedback and anecdotal evidence of your reputation, image and engagement. It's information that before now was only obtainable directly from customers or through surveys.

The benefits of monitoring include:

- See who's commenting, so you can respond in a timely way.
- See if you're getting traction – are people talking about you?
- Damage control – if people are saying negative things, you should be ready to respond, fix, etc. Social media can be an early warning system of sorts.
- Find new fans and/or people to invite to your network.
- Product or service feedback is useful for ideas, changes and product improvements.
- Save the comments in one place and see how attitudes change over time. They'll also help you interpret the numbers you're getting.[85]

Monitoring Services

2% strength	**4:1** sentiment
86% passion	**26%** reach

4 days avg. per mention

last mention 12 minutes ago

13 unique authors

10 retweets

Courtesy: socialmention

Services like Samepoint and Social Mention help track conversations. Many are free for the basic version, most are easy to use. If you're new to social media and don't have many people talking about you yet, and you have more time than money, these will probably suffice. Whether the data is useful or not depends on what you're trying to do, the accuracy with which the data is collected and how it's reported. Each site seems to have its own way of interpreting the data. For example, you'll need to check SocialMention's website to understand what they mean by "passion."

If you're looking for something more sophisticated than a DIY version, many are available, but of course they come at a price. They include: Nielson's BuzzMetrics, Overtone, tns Cymfony, ScoutLabs, among others.

Research the following to find conversations about you:

- Your company, product, service names
- Marketing messages: headlines, taglines, phrases
- Names of key people (and yourself)
- Competitor names, products, service names
- Industry keywords

Site Specific Tools

There are many tools for monitoring conversations at the specific social sites you use. For example, for Twitter, try one of the following: Chatterbox, CoTweet, Hootsuite, Splitweet and TweetBeep.

Here are a few more tips:

Trackbacks Used to notify Web authors when somebody links to one of their documents.

Hashtags Help identify Tweets related to a particular topic. Include one in a post by adding the "#" symbol in front of a word or words with no spaces, a la #yourword. Use tools like Twubs or Tagal.us to learn more about the specific meaning of a hashtag. Track them using search.twitter.com, set up a TweetDeck search for the specific word, or use tools like Tweetgrid or Twitterfall.

Adding links to Tweets is common practice, but their length can take you over the 140-character limit. Shorten them with a tool like bit.ly, which also offers tracking data.

Try It Now

1. Add tracking information to your short list of sites, focusing on the key metrics important to your business.

2. Take a measurement of where you stand today, and use this as your baseline.

3. Look up your number of inbound links.

4. Sign up for Google Maps Local.

5. Make sure you have access to your website's analytics. You may also want to sign up for Google Analytics (simply go to Google and look for the Business Solutions link in the footer).

6. While you're at it, sign up for Google Alerts to get notified when keywords or names you select appear on the Web.

7. Try out a few reputation monitoring sites and see which ones you like.

8. Periodically search for yourself on search.twitter.com and/or sign up for a Twitter dashboarding tool like TweetDeck.

9. Use any number of sites, like Technorati, Icerocket, Google Blog Search and Alltop to see if you're mentioned or to keep up with a particular topic.
10. Keep a file of running commentary and posts.
11. Determine how frequently you're going to revisit your stats.

Chapter 19: Review, Analysis & Interpretation

When it comes to marketing, you've got to track your results so you can see if what you planned actually met your objectives. Social media should be no different, but measuring its impact is an inexact science. Not unlike public relations, the numbers are open to interpretation. PR is valued, among other things, by the reputation of the medium in which the information appears, its reach, and by the amount of airtime or space it received. When an article appears in, for example a newspaper, the yardstick is column inches. The dollar value is calculated by what it would cost to run an ad of that size. As I said, not an exact science by any means. Although measurement is both art and science, it provides a way to interpret the results of your activities to determine their effectiveness.

The Big Picture

The first question is to ask if you've experienced positive growth. Some people are really focused on the number of followers they have on Twitter or the number of people in their networks. However, popularity doesn't necessarily translate into relationships or sales. The numbers are a mute point if they don't positively impact your bottom line.

Look for Change

There are many ways to interpret numbers:

*   Absolute changes in the numbers

- Percentage increases or decreases
- Changes in frequency and recency of a behavior
- Time relationships between key points, i.e., like in the purchase cycle
- Comparisons to prior time periods
- Benchmarks established by competitors or your industry

Go for Trends

Social media by its very nature is a long-term play. It's subtler than advertising and can take time to have an effect. You're building relationships, so it may not be possible to see immediate results from your efforts.

Another reason to look at trends is that it's difficult to precisely measure the return on investment from social media. As we just said about PR, one way to value a promotional activity is to calculate the comparable dollar value of another medium that has a cost associated with it. In other words, if you could say that getting fifty people to comment on your blog was equal to running an ad in a local newspaper, you would say the value of that social interaction was worth the price of that ad. For these comparisons to have any meaning, you'd have to have a more in-depth understanding of media. And even then, it's very open to interpretation. Also, since most small businesses don't have significant ad budgets, focusing on trends or increases or decreases rather than actual dollar value will tell you enough without getting overcomplicated.

Watch for Road Bumps

Be careful how you interpret the data and watch for exceptions. Unless you're getting a lot of data at once, like a high volume of traffic to your website, the single bits of information aren't going to tell you much. Trends revealed over a period of time give you a more complete picture, because one data point may be influenced by many unrelated factors. Sometimes a video is better than a snapshot.

Take the case of the guy from Italy who favorited my site on StumbleUpon. My website was getting steady traffic for months. Then one day it shot up 15 times normal. However, they were mostly tire kickers. How did I know that? From my Web stats, I could tell they didn't stay long and in most cases only visited one page. So lot's of traffic, but did it help my business? Nope. It was a bump; a wonderful ego boost, but it was unqualified traffic. As a consultant, that isn't very helpful for turning visitors into clients. Most of what I do requires me to be there in person, which is more of a local play. They'd also need to stay longer, view more pages and really get to know what I do. So, my numbers were great for that day, but not really useful for my consulting business. In other words, sometimes an unexpected increase in Web traffic is just a blip, a hiccup.

Try Different Angles and Approaches

Look at your numbers in relation to another time period, by day, month, quarter, holiday period, or year. Then think about what may have changed from one time period to the next. For example, did you increase or decrease your marketing activities? Did the health of the economy change? Did new competitors or products enter the market? Did you change your website?

Map Data to Your Marketing Activities

Check your results against your marketing activities. For example, look for spikes after posting a press release, sending out a newsletter, running an ad or joining a new social network. An easy way to keep track is to use a marketing calendar like the one described in Chapter 17 to manage key dates and scheduled marketing initiatives.

Do Post Mortems

Post mortems include data and anecdotal information about how you did on any marketing initiative. It can be a record of your investment alongside the results, so you can improve your marketing activities over time. You may even be able to calculate your ROI by comparing sales to investment. The recorded history will also be useful as you bring on new people to assist you with marketing.

Compare by Time

Create a spreadsheet or chart listing the important stats and check them periodically (weekly, monthly, quarterly), and then compare them to the previous period.

Do Some Testing

If you're already involved in a couple of social media sites, try adding a new one to your list and track your progress on that one in particular. Look for increases or decreases in activity, engagement, invitations, etc.

Compare by Social Medium or Social Site

To make sure you're spending your time on the right sites, line up the sites you participate in and compare the numbers.

Look for Changes in Behavior

Seeing how consumers interact with you on social sites will help you to realize what's working, but it will also help you understand where you might be going wrong. For example, you may be getting a lot of foot traffic in your store, but if your sales figures don't match, then perhaps they're not finding something they came in for in the first place. The same could be true on social sites – you may be getting readers and followers, but they're not clicking through to your

site. If you're participating in a social site, but no one's reacting
you're either in the wrong place or you're saying the wrong things. I
you've made sure the site you're using is well targeted, perhaps it'
what or how you're saying it. We address that next.

Part VI: Skills & Ingredients

Chapter 20: Rules of Engagement

Now that you've decided that social media makes sense for your business, you've narrowed it down to the ones you want to participate in and you know what you can do at each site, you need to know what to do once you're there. Moreover, knowing what to say and how to say it will determine its success. Laying down some ground rules, particularly if you're not the only one creating submissions, will help you stay on track.

Who Will Do the Talking?

First of all, decide who is going to be responsible for social participation in your organization. Will it be you, someone on your team, several people, are you going to hire someone? If you don't feel you're up to it or have no one in the organization to help you, consider hiring a social media consultant or community manager (CM). Consider the following checklist for selecting the right people for the job:

- Communication and writing skills
- Understand social media
- Subject matter expertise
- Functional area expertise (marketing, operations, finance, technology, etc.)
- Passion for the company and their work
- Can communicate your brand in the appropriate style, tone and voice

Once you determine who should the contributors are, be sure to identify them on your website with an image and descriptive bio. It's nice to be able to associate a face with a name.

Ground Rules

Once you pick the right people for the job, you'll want them to speak freely on your behalf without worrying that they're going to say the wrong thing. Give them rules, but allow a certain level of freedom. You'll be able to sleep at night without creating an approval bottleneck. Their communications will be much more powerful and effective if they're allowed to provide immediate, real responses to the community.

Once you create the rules, provide training for the ones who will use them. Even if you're doing this yourself, following these rules will help make your contributions more consistent:

- Set a boundary between expression and exposure — the balance between standing out as an individual, so you're memorable and interesting, and saying something that could hurt your company. It's a matter of figuring out what it's okay to say and what's not, from both a branding and legal standpoint.
- Determine the appropriate style, tone and voice (formal language, vernacular, lighthearted, serious, professional, etc.) for communicating your brand.
- Provide a clear picture of what your company's about and what you're trying to accomplish.
- Create a social media toolkit (see p. 188).
- Set time limits.

What to Say and What You Shouldn't

Once information is sent into cyberspace, it can't be erased very easily if at all. As soon as you press that "send" button, it's as good as public. And if it's been shared, there's no taking it back.

Here are some guidelines:

- Don't fake it. Don't pretend to be someone else; don't speak for someone else. The last thing you want to do is create suspicion.

- It's not advertising. Don't SPAM. If you sound like you're selling something, people will know. It's social – be social.

- Always think about why you're making the contribution, the audience and what you expect to accomplish.

- Ask yourself why the reader should be interested in what you have to say. If you're a hairstylist, help people with their frizz. Share your expertise, industry knowledge, inside information, the best places to shop, etc. Make sure you've included contact information, in case someone wants to follow up.

- Consider the ramifications of your statements before you hit send. Misplaced words could damage you or your company's hard-earned reputation. In some cases, there could be legal ramifications.

- Be natural and conversational; use an informal style, but if it's for business, keep it clean.

- When you're creating material, don't forget to include keywords, but don't use them unnaturally. If you feel you can't work them in, add tags instead.

- When making a comment, don't just say something like, "I enjoyed reading your blog post." That doesn't reveal anything about you, doesn't give anyone a reason to find out who you are, and it doesn't drive traffic to your website. Be interesting and pithy and people are more likely to follow up. The idea is to keep the conversation going.

- Don't put loaded questions (ones with an obvious ulterior motive) in question and answer areas. It's a pet peeve of mine. Maybe it works for some people, but I find it really annoying.

- Don't swear, talk too much about your personal life: "I took the kids to the park." Yawn.

Protect Your Rep

Reputation management means carefully controlling the information you put out there, and monitoring the people who are talking about you and your business. It also means preparing for the times when something goes wrong.

We can take a lesson from the crisis communication aspect of public relations when criticism and misstatements arise. If someone says something bad about you, the first step is to assess the situation: what was said and by whom, how bad it was and its potential impact. Then you'll need to decide if you should respond or ignore it. According to PR professional James E. Lukaszewski, "failure to respond and communicate in ways that meet community standards and expectations will result in a series of negative outcomes."[86]

If it has impact on your business, try to turn a negative into a positive. If possible, contact the person directly, get an understanding of the problem, resolve it, and see if you can get the person to either retract or post an update saying how their problem was resolved.

Another option is to crowd out the negative comments by making sure you have enough good comments to outweigh the bad, because many sites show the most recent ones first. As time goes on, the old, bad comments drop to the bottom and recede into the past.

Don't dismiss all negative reviews or complaints as illegitimate, however. Some people may have a point, and you may want to review your business practices to see what can be improved. Be thankful for the free research.

If you need to make a more public response as opposed to a specific individual, Lukaszewski includes these suggestions for dealing with the problem:

Candor Acknowledge the problem promptly and publicly and that something will be done to remedy the situation.

Explanation Explain what happened, talk about what was learned and how it will influence your company's behavior in the future, and commit to providing updates until the crises is resolved.

Declaration Make a public commitment to positive steps to address the issues and to resolve the situation.

Contrition Verbalize your "regret, empathy, sympathy, even embarrassment."

Restitution "Pay the price" quickly and exceed expectations. "Adverse situations remediated quickly cost far less and are controversial for much shorter periods of time."

Chapter 21: The Social Media Toolkit

The social media toolkit is designed to help you organize your contributions and communicate consistently. It should be shared with all of your contributors. Keep the information and materials in a binder and/or folder on your computer, so you can access it at any time. Your toolkit may include:

Objectives Remind yourself why you're participating and what you want to get across.

Rules of engagement As described in Chapter 20.

Keywords As described on page 19.

Business description Have descriptions of your business available in various lengths, i.e., short, medium, long, because every social site sets different limitations for this feature.

Important Web addresses Keep a list of all your properties' URL's and RSS/xml feeds.

Social list Prioritize your list of social sites by type and importance. Be sure to keep logins and passwords handy, but in a safe place. Try to map the connections between them, although I have to admit that's not an easy exercise.

Visual identity Some sites allow you to customize the "skin" or the look and feel of your profile. Options may include: adding a logo, changing colors or fonts, adding badges or widgets, even repositioning content. Not all social sites allow you to do this, but it's nice to have the elements handy for when you can.

Messaging Key ideas or statements about your company that reference your core competencies, products and positioning.

Key phrases should be used judiciously, or you'll sound like an advertisement. The key concepts should remain the same for consistency, but don't need to be said the same way every time.

Naming conventions Determine the name people will use when participating. For business, use the participant's real name or company name. However, company names are not generally recommended for individual conversations, because that's rather impersonal. A company name may be used for the name of a property, like a Facebook page or Twitter account. Personal users may choose to use an alias, but lack of transparency may create distrust on the part of the reader.

Contacts Keep a list of the places where you have your contacts, like personal address books, your contact manager, LinkedIn, Google Mail, etc. It will come in handy when you're ready to invite people to your networks.

Assets Keep track of your assets, like articles, images, video, audio, podcasts, etc. Use a tool like Google's Picasa or Flickr for images.

Tracking mechanisms Select from the list of tracking tools discussed in Chapter 18, and determine which reports you're going to gather on a regular basis.

Try It Now

1. Think about creating your own rules of engagement and place them in priority order.

2. Create your own social media toolkit.

3. Check on review sites related to your business to see if you're mentioned and what people are saying about you. Is there anything that needs repair?

4. Be prepared to manage negative comments by anticipating what they may be. List complaints you think people may have down one side of a sheet of paper, and write down what you might say or do to resolve them on the other.

Chapter 22: Submissions & Posts

Submissions and posts take two forms. One is the more immediate, off-the-cuff remark posted on the walls of social networks, in comment areas and on microblogs. The other is the well-considered, longer form, like a blog entry or article. What you contribute depends on its purpose, time-sensitivity, subject, and your time and skill.

Basic Structure

In either case, the structure is basically the same. Some longer formats, like the social media press release[87] or story, are the exception. You'll need the following:

	Structure of a Submission		
Subject Line	Give 'Em the Goods	Wrap It Up	Point to Your Site
Hook & Peg	Just the info they're looking for	Summary Conclusion Twist Recommendations Next steps	Link to your site Give them a reason to visit

Subject line Headline, hook, peg, benefit, WIIFM.

Give them the goods You need to teach, inform, help, explain, surprise, excite, or provide insight. Offer news, how-to's, explain a process, describe a character, give relevant details, make it emotional, controversial, or offer an opinion.

Respond to blog posts or articles by offering an opinion of substance – add an insight, find, news or statistic. It will be more useful or interesting, and therefore more likely to be published and shared. People will be more engaged and they may even follow up with a comment of their own. Getting people to respond shows they're paying attention.

Wrap it up Summary, conclusions, twist, recommendations, next steps.

Provide a compelling reason to go to your website, if appropriate. Add an incentive, such as the promise of more in-depth information, free download, discount or contest. Give a reason to act quickly, such as a deadline, expiration date, or limited availability.

Link Many sites will automatically link to your Web address (or the link you included in your profile). If they don't, it's up to you to provide contact information. Most sites don't mind if you do, but not all (some sites don't like to send visitors off their sites, and they'll let you know this). If you're not sure, try it, and if you get a warning don't do it again. You could get banned from the site for good.

Hook & Peg

If you want to make any headway at all, you've got to grab the attention of the reader. That's what the headline, hook, benefit and peg are for. The headline should interest the reader by including something that connects with what they care about. They can relate to it. You're giving them a reason to read the information you're providing. Make it useful or be ignored. It's what's known as the WIIFM or the "What's In It For Me" approach.

Hooks			
Informational	**News**	**Humor**	**Evil**
Tips, hints and tricks, or a personal experience	Fresh information that will spread	Funny story Joke Anecdote Bizarre picture	Negative opinion, but with evidence to back it up

Timeliness is another way to grab attention. Known as a peg, it's the "why you're telling me this now" – in other words, you're pegging it to some current news, event, happening or whatever. It provides relevance and context to what you're going to say. And information that's relevant to the reader is more likely to be read.

Chapter 23: Food for Thought

The whole point of social media is to provide something useful to the reader, not to sell them. If you sound like that, people will get turned off because they expect to be informed, entertained, invited or inspired – not be sold to. If you are trying to make a sale directly, take advantage of a social site's advertising opportunities.

It's kind of like the life insurance salesperson stepping into a roomful of business professionals who are at the event to make connections, but not to buy insurance – or anything else for that matter for their personal use. On the other hand, don't talk business on a site designed for consumers. It will be out of context and possibly annoy people in your network. You'll come across as a social doofus. This can happen inadvertently, however, if your accounts are automatically sharing posts. I often see business-related Tweets appearing on Facebook for example.

Here are a few more ideas on what to write:

- Tips or checklists
- Answer questions
- Ask a question readers can't help but want an answer to
- Provide advice and information
- Describe a personal experience
- Create an expert round-up
- Provide or link to industry stats
- Create intrigue by hinting at something bigger or to come
- Start a heated debate

For even more ideas, try buying a collection of magazines you think your audience reads. Look at the cover and how the writers entice people into reading what's inside. Look over the table of contents for subjects you can write about, but use your own voice and experiences. Go to the publications' websites and review their editorial calendars to see what they're planning on writing about in the future.

Case Studies

Write about clients or people you've had contact with and explain a situation: describe the problem, what you did and the results. Get permission to use real names. If you can't, speak about the case generically, describing rather than referring to actual people. Be original and if appropriate, make it personal.

Get People to Read Your Stuff Checklist

- Whatever you do, write for the audience.
- Make sure what you're saying is worth reading or listening to.
- Consider their point of view and their WIIFM.
- Be compelling by being relevant (to the time and the reader).
- Use creative language and drama to get noticed – take creative risks.
- Use honest language.
- Use terminology the reader understands and cares about.
- Be concise. Be interesting, but when you can't – be brief.
- Avoid clichés and generalities.
- Illustrate your point with words and stories. Use actual pictures when appropriate.
- Be objective or controversial (carefully; realize your impact).
- Create contrast.
- Get help with writing or editing if you need it.
- Proofread!
- Optimize with keywords.

Chapter 24: Managing Your Time

So how do you keep control of it all? As I've been saying throughout the book, you need to think strategically. That's the biggest time saver there is. But here are some concrete tips you can put into practice.

Be Choosy

Don't use every social tool. Pick the right mainstream site(s), and then choose the top 3-5 niche sites using the methods described in this book. Track your results. If nothing's happening on one, knock it off the list, then focus on the remaining ones, or add another to the list and see how that goes.

Control the Flow

At the social sites you belong to, set your account's email preferences to manage what gets sent to your inbox. Rather than choosing to receive just any email, be selective. Notifications can be important for responding in a timely manner, but you can just log in occasionally to check other activity.

Leverage Web-Mail

Use the email tools described on page 45 to make it faster and easier to invite people to your networks.

Post on High Traffic Sites

Creating your own properties can be a good strategy, but will require you to build traffic of your own. If you have no visitors, it's not going to be a very social place. It might be better to hang out at other sites with more sociability to leverage their traffic. Take advantage of Site Swag (described on page 120).

Set Limits

Get a timer or set alarms on your computer. If there's something better you can be doing to promote your business, set the clock, let's say, for two :30 minute intervals per day and let it go at that. If social media is working for you, increase it. If not, decrease it.

Do the Q&A

Get the word out easily through Question and Answer areas on the sites where your audience hangs out. Search for questions related to your product or expertise, and provide tips, tools and solutions.

Sites like Askforia and WikiAnswers specialize in sharing knowledge through Q&A's.

Show Don't Tell

The Web is a visual medium and there are lots of opportunities to communicate without words, so don't always think written material first. Next time you want to voice an opinion, think about using images, video and/or audio to tell your story.[88]

Recently, I was going to write a blog post about an event I attended in Seattle. I had taken a series of pictures, and I wanted to share my marketing point of view about how the event was managed. The prospect of writing a blog entry was a bit daunting with everything else I had to do that day. So instead, I posted the images to Flickr, wrote comments for each photo, and then linked to it from Twitter. It was easy to do, and created a different kind of experience for the viewer – probably a bit more fun than reading another article. I could have created a slideshow as well to post on a content site like SlideShare.

Cross-Pollinate

Posting the same information on all your social media sites can be very time consuming, but there are tools that help you do some of the sharing automatically.

The following will help you connect, interconnect, extend your presence, and grow your popularity:

- Link all your social profiles into one place with AtomKeep. Create an online business card with card.ly.
- Ping.fm allows you to post updates from anywhere to anywhere.
- Use Facebook applications to pull information from other social networks, as appropriate.
- Use the hashtags #in or #li to selectively share Tweets with your LinkedIn status. Or use #fb for Facebook.

- Flickr is integrated with many social networks, but it will also help you share your images with all kinds of sites like TypePad, Blogger, LiveJournal and FriendFeed.
- Dropico will let you share photos across social networks.
- Yahoo's Upcoming shares event data with many other sites.
- Rather than adding lots of links to your site, SocialFollow helps you create one button that links people to all your social networks.

If you decide to share your posts among different sites, be sure that what you write in one is appropriate for the other. In other words, you could be posting something personal to Facebook about a party you attended. If your Facebook account is linked to a business site, that could be awkward. Plus in many cases the format may not work. For example, you may be able to write a lengthy post in one place, but Twitter only picks up 140 characters.

Use Dashboards

Dashboards give you a quick snapshot of what's happening in your online world. Make use of Google Analytic's dashboard to monitor website traffic. Sign up for TweetDeck or something like it to monitor Twitter. Use a lifestreaming tool, like FriendFeed or Silentale, to bring all your social interactions into one place.

If you're feeling ambitious, create your own social media dashboard with iGoogle, Netvibes or Pageflakes to monitor the sites, subjects, categories and keywords related to your business. They allow you to bring in RSS feeds from the sites you've chosen to monitor.

Part VII: Where Do We Go from Here?

Trends & Predictions

Chapter 25: Trends & Predictions

It's a little weird to talk about the future of social media, consid ering that there's so little past, but every day seems to bring a new tool, idea or application. The rate at which new ways to communicate are proliferating is making more than a few marketers a little crazy. Everyone's running around trying to figure out how to use it, justify ing it to their bosses or clients, and wondering whether there's really an ROI or not. With social media conversations fragmenting the con sistent messages promoters are trying to put out there, and the speed at which news travels, everything is getting more and more complex and in a way, spinning out of control.

I hope this book has put some rationality on the subject, but it's just a snapshot of what exists today. Change is inevitable as new technologies are developed and existing ones, like RFID and text-to speech (Twitterfone already lets users send Twitter updates using voice), are integrated into social media. I'm not a technologist, so I won't try to predict what the new technologies will be. Instead, I'll focus on the changing attitudes and evolution of the marketplace – at least for the near future. Change is also inevitable as social media evolves, the population ages and social butterflies flit to the next ex citing thing.

Changing Demographics

Social media may have started as a way for young people to con nect, but they're certainly not the only ones using it today. Although not the majority, the fastest growing user group is aged 55 and over. "In addition to participating in the more established social networks, older users are also carving out their own niche online with websites such as Eons, EldersVoice, TeeBeeDee and BOOMj."[89] Some predict that over time the demographics of social media users will reflect the general population of Web users. What this means for businesses is that social media may become as necessary for reaching most audi ences as having a website.

Verging on Real Life

The more social media reflects real life, becoming part of everything we do, the more useful it becomes. It's already a part of our digital lives – at home on our computers, converging with TV and on our mobile devices. As the new technologies proliferate and prices fall, more people will be able to afford it and find ways to use it. Behaviors will change. It will become natural to check a review site for a restaurant or look for friends to meet up with at the movies. Friends will send recommendations just as they near the theater. The possibilities are almost endless as more data is tracked, technology changes and marketers find new ways to capitalize on what the geeks have created.

Everyone's a Critic

Our typical filters are fading fast. It used to be when you wanted to buy something, you'd read *Consumer Reports*, check your local newspaper or yellow pages or read a restaurant critic's advice. As newspapers consolidate and close and magazines get thinner, thanks in part to more and more user-generated content (Craigslist has decimated newspaper classified advertising for example), you may not be able to continue getting your information that way even if you wanted to.

User-generated doesn't mean the opinions are unbiased, however. In fact, it's probably the opposite. It seems like standards are fading and the bar is dropping ever lower. Anyone can voice an opinion on the Web – that doesn't mean they know what they're talking about. Some might say that on balance the good will rise to the top, but that means it's a popularity contest. And popularity doesn't have a good rep for being a measure of quality.

Ratings often average out; half like that restaurant, half don't, so you need to read each commentary to form your own opinion about their opinions. That's a lot of work. We're already experiencing information overload. My hope is that people will still want quality information from the experts, like restaurant review service Zagat or Metacritic which combines public and expert criticism. On the other hand, experts can't always keep up, like with the explosion of self-published books. So Shelfari became the place to talk about them.

Changes in Media Consumption

There are only so many hours in the day and our time is increasingly fractionalized. Add social media to the pile of radio, TV, mp3 players, mobile devices, video and the Web, and something's gotta give.

Remember the time before cable when there were only 3 channels (okay, I'm old). Then how about the time before the Web or email existed? What did we do with ourselves? And now we have social media. "Two-thirds of the world Internet population participates in social networking or blogging sites. This utilization represents almost 10% of all Internet time around the world."[90] People are spending more of their personal time online with their social networks than checking or writing email.[91] What's next? Soon, we'll all be so jacked in there won't be time for any real experiences at all. Or, social media will hit a ceiling because people will still want real interaction – ultimately making it an enabler, not a replacement.

Media consumption has increased, yet television remains in the lead. According to a 2008 report, "...the average Nielsen household watched more than 151 hours of television per month. Internet users logged on for 27 viewing hours a month and mobile subscribers consumed nearly four hours of video on a mobile phone and almost three hours on the Internet."[92] All this wouldn't be possible without multitasking. Almost a third of someone's Internet time is spent simultaneously watching TV.[93] Maybe the final frontier is media while you sleep.

> The final frontier: media while you sleep.

There's a lot of media shape shifting going on, too. People are choosing *when* they watch TV with digital video recorders (known as "time-shifting), and *where* with mobile devices and the Net. As more video, TV and radio go online, media will continue to change. Computers have already replaced radio as the second most popular medium.[94]

Another growing trend is the rise of "telecommunities" or groups of people who watch TV while chatting online in real time. It's affecting how people watch TV. "Video Villages" have been shown to spend more time watching a program.[95] "Telecommunity members who connected via Facebook during the Oscars were online for 76 minutes and watched 50% more of the broadcast than the average Academy Award viewer. Twitter reported more than 100,000 Oscar-related 'tweets' during the broadcast, an astonishing 400 messages per minute."[96]

Social Media on the Move

With so many people getting used to accessing and using information whenever and wherever they want, it just makes sense that social media has made its way to wireless devices. Usage is growing fast. As of June 2007, 12.3 million consumers in the U.S. and Western Europe used mobile phones to access social networks. If mobile usage in European markets is any indication of U.S. trends, which it has been, mobile social networking will continue to grow. eMarketer forecasts it will increase from 82 million users in 2007 to over 800 million worldwide by 2012.

Beyond the use of mobile for voice, information delivered via mobile includes text messaging, multimedia, applications, games and Web pages (through a mobile browser, like Safari on the iPhone). When it comes to marketing, mobile delivers alerts, sales materials, coupons and advertising. The only real difference between a mobile device and a computer is the smaller viewing screen and generally slower delivery speed (which is at least partly dependent on the available bandwidth).

The iPhone has driven the growth of mobile social networks, but what someone does while mobile depends on the applications available on their device and their ability to access the Internet, which requires a data plan from a wireless provider (sometimes users can tap into a WiFi connection). The exception is text messaging, which is universally available on most, if not all, mobile devices. This may be partly responsible for the rapid growth of text-based Twitter.

Despite these limitations, more and more people are accessing social media via mobile. It's second only in popularity to news and information as the reason for accessing the Internet via handsets.[97] While it's true that more people have mobile devices than computers and mobile Internet usage is increasing, only about 20% of mobile subscribers in the U.S. access the Web via mobile.[98] That "only" is still more than 50 million people. As mobile Internet access increases, there's little doubt that social media accessed this way will continue to rise. For young users, the mobile phone has become more central to their way of life – especially their social lives.[99]

People who are social while mobile are updating their status, posting to blogs, Tweeting, playing social games and checking their Facebook accounts, and it doesn't really matter if they're at home, in the car or out and about. However, context can be important. Delivering information where they are at a specific moment makes it more relevant. Consider the traveler at an airport, on a train, in a car, or even walking. They may need the information right then – like knowing if the friend who is picking them up is stuck in traffic. Or consider delivering a coupon to a shopper, helping them find the store in a mall and connecting them with a friend to help them choose the right item.

Beyond the pure utility, people use mobile social media when they're bored or lonely, waiting in line or simply thinking about friends, family and colleagues. People still kill time playing games, but now they're likely to play them with their social networks.

Another strength of mobile is the built-in GPS, which places the device in a relatively specific location and allows developers to create applications based on where the user is at any time. Consider the student looking for nearby friends to play a pickup game after class. Or a user who's en route to a party and needs to pick up a bottle of wine or a last minute gift. Perhaps they're out shopping and want to know the reviews for a particular toaster that's on sale. Before, a mapping application tied to where they are at that moment would have been useful information. Now it's made even more useful with recommendations from a review site.

Mobile is a key feature of Twitter, but many other mainstream social sites have incorporated a mobile component. Facebook and LinkedIn give iPhone users access to their social networks while out and about. That's important, because adults are expected to increase their use of mobile social media for professional networking as their use of text messaging increases.[100]

There are dozens of social network sites you can access from your mobile phone, and that number will surely grow. New mobile tools are being created every day. ShoZu, Cliqset and Kinoma Play connect users with their networks to share media from their handsets. Aloqa lets users know which of their friends and favorite spots are nearby. Brightkite offers location-based social networking.

If your business appeals to these types of customers, you'll want to make sure you tap into the social tools that get you into their mobile hands. As this space evolves, it may not even matter whether people have the choice between a computer and a mobile device. They may simply choose to do everything on their handsets.

As more people get social while mobile, it's becoming more important to make company websites viewable on the small screen. Create a mobile website without programming using a tool like Wirenode or Jag.ag, or make your existing website mobile-friendly with Mofuse.

Social Utility

I've already mentioned, and it's already happening of course, that social media is likely to become a common utility, just as ecommerce or email has, since the tools make it fairly simple. There's going to be a bit of social in everything.

In some cases, blog formats have overtaken the typical website form, with many integrating seamlessly with other social sites. Tools used for building websites are beginning to include social tools, as well. All this could mean that social interactions may become just as ubiquitous as a contact page on a website.

In addition, as media entities, like television networks and magazines, make social components standard on their websites, standalone niche social sites may find it more difficult to compete with these content-rich, well-marketed powerhouses.

User Burnout

The social media picture may not be as rosy as the hype makes it out to be, but the data is conflicted. On one hand, there's some indication that time spent on social sites is declining, although record numbers of middle-aged people are joining. On the other hand, some are saying that there are fewer overall visits to social sites, but the people who are still going spend more time on them.

I'm already hearing that people are tired of Facebook, finding it a waste of time and barely visiting the site. Some have called this "Facebook fatigue"[101] as people tire of the endless friend requests, and perhaps realize that the two-dimensional conversations aren't as exciting as the real thing. There are other plausible explanations, like the novelty has worn off, the experience isn't worth it, boredom or even a backlash against the lack of privacy.

Facebook fatigue may provide some insight into why people will spend less time on that site, but it may also explain why people are beginning to spend more time on niche sites they find more useful, interesting or geared towards their particular interests. Niche sites may have a better chance to develop a loyal following for a number of reasons: they deliver useful content, have interesting and influential members and they provide an easier way for members to be noticed.[102]

In addition, college graduates who had spent a lot of time on Facebook when they were at school may be slowing their mingling as they spend more time at work and have less time for social sites. And as their parents and grandparents join the network where they shared their party news and exploits, they may feel the need to seek out networks of their peers — at least until they're ready to announce their weddings.

These changes in behavior will also have an impact on the way businesses use social media for promotional purposes. As time goes on and more data comes in, it will be interesting to see if social media maintains its status and where it ultimately gets placed among other marketing methods.

Lifecycle of Social Media

Despite the potential user burnout, it looks like social media is here to stay — for users anyway; maybe not for the social sites themselves — at least the ones trying to make a living at it. Most social sites haven't been able to figure out a sustainable revenue model beyond advertising. So far, many are surviving through venture funding.

As the space matures, there will be increasing competition and diversification as social sites compete for share of audience. With all the new tools, there are few barriers to creating a site, but the real work is in continuing to attract, interest and engage audiences. It also means marketing them to increase the size of the network and its usage.

Consolidation among the mainstream will probably continue, as there seems to be room for only a few at the top of any particular social media type. This could be because users choose their favorites and stay with them. The site gains traction and gets sticky. In other words, the "switching cost" is high. Users get comfortable being on a site where their friends are and it gets increasingly difficult to change to a new one. Once a site hits critical mass, it has a momentum of its own. But even the giants can stumble as new players enter the fray. Facebook trouncing Myspace is a perfect example.

Why some sites survive, while others meet their demise is somewhat of a mystery. It isn't easy to predict that path to greatness. For example, YouTube has risen to the top in popularity among hundreds of other video sites. Why? Perhaps it gained momentum simply because it was easier to use. Media hype helped, and I'm convinced the name had a lot to do with it. Twitter is a more recent example. It beat out Jaiku, Utterly and Pownce. Once Twitter took hold, the others just couldn't compete with the market leader. Utterz has since become Utterli and changed its business model to allow people to share files via mobile. Pownce has since shut down.

Although users may ultimately choose only a few mainstream sites, that doesn't mean they won't participate in any number of niche sites, depending on their needs and interests. Just like magazines, there's a social site for every taste, style and topic. Perhaps social sites will become little micro-neighborhoods, but that's going to make it awfully hard to gain enough audience to survive on advertising revenue. Perhaps new dashboard-like tools will come along that will be better at aggregating ones social world, so a person can follow as many sites as they have interests.

As the number of niche sites continues to grow, competition will become more intense. This will cause the sites and the social tools that support them to seek differentiated business models. The social market as a result will become increasingly fragmented and verticalized around specific industries and audiences.

Rate of Technological Change

I said I wasn't going to try to predict what's next for technology, but if the past is any indication, change will come faster and faster. Old tech will be replaced by the next innovation, and before you know it, someone will come up with the next disruptive idea. When kids are creating software in their bedrooms, a garage is no longer needed to start a band and movies can be shot with a cellphone, what's next?

No matter what changes come along though, one thing is certain. Human behavior, in terms of how people want to connect with each other, hasn't evolved all that much. And that means the marketing fundamentals still apply. At the end of the day, we're still all social animals who are open to new ideas and toys, ways of looking at the world, and ultimately persuasion. That hasn't changed much.

SOURCES

Listed below are sites and tools I referenced in the text, as well as others that supplied data or influenced my thoughts on the topic. Some of the tools may not work perfectly because they're new and in beta, but they're worth a try.

All are .com unless otherwise noted
For more tools and resources, visit blockbeta.com

Cases

Amazon	Guinness
Angie's List	ELance
BaconSalt	Salesforce
Cadbury-Schweppes Stride	Zappos
Chewing Gum	
Craigslist	

For more social media case studies, visit MarketingSherpa.

Research

AllYouCanRead	Nielsen
Bizshark	PEW Internet Research
DoshDosh	PR-squared for their social me-
eMarketer	dia press release
Findasocialnetwork	Search Engine Watch
Forrester	Socialnetworklist
Google BlogSearch	U.S. Census
Internet Advertising Bureau:	World-Newspapers
IAB.com	
Mashable: Social Media Guide	
Mintel	

Social Sites

Alltop
Amazon
Askforia
BakeSpace
Barbie
Biznik
BoomBang
BoomJ
CafeMom
ClassmatesOnline
ClubPenguin
Delicious
Digg
Disney
Eons
Etsy
Eventful
EveryBlock
Facebook
Flickr

LinkedIn
Meetup
Metacritic
Myarchn
MySpace
Naymze
Nickelodeon
Outside.in
Patch
Plaxo
PodcastAlley
SeattleTechStart-
ups
SecondLife
Shelfari
SlideShare
Spoke
Squidoo
Stumbleupon
StyleHive

TeachStreet
Technorati
TeeBeeDee
The Knot
TripAdvisor
Twitter
Upcoming
Webkinz
WikiCompany.org
WikiHow
Wikia
WikiAnswers:
wiki.answers.com
WikiMapia
Wikipedia
Wikitravel.org
Xing
Yelp
YouTube

Supporting Sites

AddThis
ArticlesBase
AtomKeep
Bloglink (Linke-
dIn)
CommonCraft
DappFactory:
dapper.net/open
GetSatisfaction

Google: Adwords,
Calendar
Groupon
MatchboxCalendar
Meebo
OfferPalMedia
OnlyWire
Ping.fm
Pingomatic
PRLeap

PRWeb
ShareThis
Simpletracks:
kalsey.com/tools/t
rackback
ThomasNet
TripIt

Twitter

Chatterbox.hq.com
CoTweet
FriendorFollow
Hootsuite
Klout
Listorious
SocialOomph
Splitweet
Tagal.us
TweetDeck
Twitip

Twitter
Tweepler
TweetBeep
TweetCloud
Tweetdeck
Tweetgrid
Twitterfall
Twitterfone
TwitterFox
TwitterGroups

TwitterKarma:
dossy.org/twitter/
karma
Twitterless
Twitterly
Twitter Search:
search.twitter.com
Twtpoll
Twubs

Tracking, Monitoring & Dashboards

Tracking & Monitoring

Alexa
Bantam:
bantamlive.com
Brightkite
Cliqset
Compete
Friendfeed
Google: Alerts,
Analytics, Web-
master Tools
Ice Rocket:
trend.icerocket.co
m

Lexicon:
facebook.com/lexi
con
Nielson's Buzz-
Metrics:
nielson-online.com
Overtone
PRChecker.info
Quantcast
Samepoint
ScoutLabs
Silentale
Simpletracks:
kalsey.com/tools/t
rackback
Social Mention
Socrata

tns Cymfony:
cymfony.com
WhoLinksToMe
Yahoo's Site Ex-
plorer:
siteexplorer.search.
yahoo.com

Dashboards

Bloglines
iGoogle
Netvibes
Pageflakes

Properties & Widgets

Blogger
Clearspring
CommonCraft
CreativeCommons
DappFactory:
dapper.net
Google: Friend-
Connect
Gydget
KickApps

Lijit
Ning
Opensocial.org
SocialGo
Squarespace
Squidoo
Typepad
Wetpaint
WidgetBox
Wikia

WordPress
Yahoo Pipes
Yammer
YouTube Channels
Zembly

Email

AWeber
ConstantContact
MyEmma
RatePoint

StrongMail
VerticalResponse

Mobile

Aloqa
Jag.ag
Kinoma
Mofuse
ShoZu
Wirenode

GLOSSARY

Listed below are some of the terms used in this book to describe social media and marketing. For more glossaries and information, visit: IAB.net, Webopedia or Wikipedia.

Advertorial
Paid advertising that contains editorial-like content.

Affinity and Affinity Groups
People with similar interests who congregate in one place, like in chat rooms, on discussion boards or on social networks. A community of people sharing a common culture.

Aggregator
An organization that creates collections of feeds.

Algorithm
Generally a formula used to solve a math or computing problem, and used by search engines to rank results. The calculation takes into account many factors, like where keywords appear and inbound links to a website.

API (Application Programming Interface)
An API allows one software application to interact with another. They include instructions for software developers, defining how information needs to be exchanged between them. An API may specify routines, data structures, object classes and protocols. These instructions are often found in the "developer toolkit" found on a software company's website.

Avatar
An image used to represent a computer user; often used as a replacement for a photo.

Badge
A graphic image or icon provided by a social site to represent a membership, accomplishment or other behavior.

Bizographics (AKA firmographics)
Similar to demographics, which are the characteristics of an individual, bizographics define an organization and the people who fall within a target profile.

Bot
A small computer program used to search the Web automatically.

Browser
Software used to read Web pages; popular versions include: Chrome, Firefox, Flock (integrates social tools), Internet Explorer, Opera and Safari.

Channel
Organizations involved in getting a product to market, from supplier to manufacturer to distributor to wholesaler to retailer, and anyone in between. May also be used to define the medium used to convey information, as in a communications channel.

Chiclet
A small icon indicating the availability of an RSS feed; typically found on a blog or Web page.

Clutter
An overabundance of advertising messages that obscures a specific message.

CMS (Content Management System)
Software used for storing, controlling, revising, and publishing Web sites.

Collateral

Any type of printed materials used for marketing, such as business cards, brochures, sales sheets, fliers, etc.

Column Inches (CI)

A typical unit of measure for newspapers. A CI is one column wide by one inch high. In the U.S., newspapers are six columns wide with a standard column width of about 1 and 13/16 inches.

Cookie

In computing, a small piece of text stored on a user's computer by a web browser; may identify user preferences, shopping cart contents, session information, or other data used by websites. Each time a browser connects with a website's server, a cookie is sent to the browser. Cookies may be used to track users as they visit various sites. Users can choose to accept or reject them, although rejecting cookies can render some sites unusable. Some shopping carts or login systems, for example, require cookies to work properly.

Crowdsource

The idea that a group of people can do a job typically done by an employee or contractor. On the Web, an open request is made and anyone can respond. May be used for brainstorming, market research, design or to carry out particular tasks.

Dashboard

An interface that makes it easy to manage data from several sources by bringing it into one place. Dashboards may be used to show website traffic statistics or feeds from several social sites.

Developer Toolkit

See API

Differentiation

In marketing, it's what sets a business apart from the competition. Differentiation value may be found in products and services, pricing, distribution or the way a business promotes itself and provides a strategic advantage.

Download (also see Upload)

Transferring a file from a computer.

Downstream (also see Upstream)

The sites a visitor goes to next after visiting a website.

Embed

When a bit of code is injected into a Web page for the purpose of placing content, like a video or slideshow. Applications, like widgets, may be embedded, too.

Favorite

Either a browser bookmark saved as a shortcut to a website; or an object someone saves to their profile on a social site, as in favorite people, videos or articles.

Feed

Often associated with RSS. Publishers create feeds to share their content as it's updated. Subscribers to the feed read it using a feed reader or newsreader. A feed reader is software that aggregates content into one place for easy viewing. The user subscribes to a feed by entering the feed's URL or by clicking an RSS icon. The reader then updates the feeds as new information is published.

Folksonomy (AKA, collaborative tagging, social classification, social indexing, and social tagging)

A system used to create and manage tags to organize content.

Gadget (also see Widget)
A small bit of code placed on a website to perform a specific, novelty function.

Halo Effect
The perception someone has of something or someone based on the context within which they experience it.

Hashtag
A word or words (no spaces) with the symbol "#" in front of it. Used on Twitter to identify Tweets related to a specific topic.

Host (AKA Web Host)
A service that runs Internet servers, which provide the means for delivering content to the Internet. Other services may include email, ecommerce functionality and website builders.

HTML (HyperText Markup Language)
The main language and coding scheme used to create Web pages. It consists of tags (not to be confused with keyword tags) that determine how a page should look. The format of a tag is <object>. For example, the tag for placing an image is <img>.

Impression
The appearance of an advertisement on a Web page.

IP Address (Internet Protocol Address)
A number representing a device accessing the Internet and its virtual location. The typical format is: 123.45.678.910

Keyword
Words used to search for information online. Authors may anticipate the keywords searchers use, and create one, two or three word phrases to include in their content so they may be located.

Lifestreaming
An online tool that aggregates all social interactions into one place.

Linkbait
Content that is created for the purpose of attracting other websites to link to it.

Lurk
Hanging out on a social site without being identified.

Mashup
A web page or application that combines data or functionality not usually found together from two or more outside sources to create a new service. For example, it's common to combine maps with neighborhood information.

Metatag
HTML or XHTML element providing additional information about a Web page. It's placed at the top of the page, but is hidden from view of the website visitor. Can be used to provide a page description, keywords or other information not included in other attributes. At one point, were significant in achieving optimal search engine results, but this isn't the case anymore. Other characteristics like incoming links from related high traffic websites, quantity and quality of content, functional links, viewer traffic, time spent on a site and freshness have become more significant in determining rank.

MSA (Metropolitan Statistical Area)
U.S. government classification for a free-standing urban area.

Narrowcast
Transmitting information to a select group of recipients, like sending an email newsletter to a customer list.

Organic Search
Results shown on search engines based on relevance to terms or keywords, rather than on pay-per-click advertising.

Out-of-Home
Advertising that reaches someone anywhere outside the home, such as billboards, shopping carts, digital signs, etc.

PageRank
Google's linking algorithm for ranking the relative importance of websites on a scale from 1-10. It's based on the number of credible inbound links a site has. A site's PageRank helps determine where a site appears in Google search results.

Pay-Per-Click (PPC)
A type of digital advertising where the advertiser pays when an ad is selected by clicking on it.

Pay-Per-Performance (PPP)
A type of advertising where the advertiser only pays for measurable results, like a sale.

Permalink
Common to blogging, a URL that remains unchanged and points to a specific blog or forum entry, even after it is no longer current. They're useful, because people often want to link to particular content or articles. When Web content was static, all links were permanent. Now, with so much content delivered dynamically, there arose a need for fixed URL's. Many, but not all, blogging systems support them.

Ping
A mechanism through which a blog notifies a server that its content has been updated. For example, pingomatic let's search engines know

when a blog has been updated. Ping.fm is used to update social networks.

Plugin (AKA add-in, add-on, snap-in, and sometimes extension)
A computer program that interacts with an application, such as a Web browser, to provide specific functionality.

Podcast
A digital media file, or series of files, residing at a unique web feed address and distributed over the internet for playback on portable media players or computers. The term is a combination of "broadcast" and "pod."

Portal
A website organizing and presenting information from many sources in a consistent way. Web portals offer other services, such as Web mail, news, financial reporting and more.

Positioning
The place an entity (person, product, service or organization) occupies in a prospect's mind.

Property
A digital entity, such as a website, blog, email signature, Facebook Page or social network, "owned" by their creators.

Qualified Leads
Prospects who have an interest in purchasing a business's products or services. Usually fit a predefined target profile.

Retweet
To share a Twitter post.

RSS (Really Simple Syndication)

A way for authors to publish frequently updated works—such as blog entries, news headlines, audio, and video—in a standardized format known as XML. XML allows the information to be repurposed for many different formats and programs known as feeds. Readers can subscribe to them to stay informed as information is updated, or to bring information into one place, as on a dashboard. RSS feeds can be read using a feed reader on the Web, a computer or mobile device.

Search Bots

See bots

Segmentation

Method used to define prospects along selected characteristics and similar behaviors. It's a practical way to target more precisely, but not have to implement separate marketing approaches for each individual.

SEM (Search Engine Marketing)

Any type of Internet marketing designed to increase website visibility on search engine results pages (SERPs).

SEO (Search Engine Optimization)

Increasing the likelihood that a website will appear favorably on a search engine results page by building it to accommodate the way these search engines look for information.

SERP (Search Engine Results Page)

The Web page produced by a search engine when a visitor uses words to find information.

Server (AKA Web server)
A computer that delivers Web pages and other services, like email streaming audio or instant messaging, after a request is made from a browser.

Session (AKA User Session)
Period in which a user (with a unique IP address) interacts with a website.

Site Swag
Places on a website where a visitor may participate or add information for free, and therefore take advantage of it for promotional purposes. May include: directories, Q&A's, blog comments, press release posts, etc.

Smartphone
A mobile phone with the addition of computer-like capabilities, like email and the ability to access the Internet.

Social Capital
Value derived from social network connections.

Social Search
When someone uses their online social network to get information like advice, recommendations or referrals.

Spider (AKA Web Crawler)
A type of bot that browses the Web in a methodical, automated manner called Web crawling or spidering. Specifically used by search engines to stay updated.

Stickiness
When a website visitor returns to a site repeatedly, views several pages or stays for a certain length of time. It's one way to measure the value of social media.

Switching Cost
What a user has to give up to change to a new social site.

Tag
Words a participant can add to their comments or content which make them searchable. Many sites allow users to select from a list of pre-existing words or to add their own.

Tag Cloud (AKA Word Cloud)
A group of words graphically represented, which appear on many social sites. The size and color of the words reflect how often they're used in the social content of a site. They're often clickable, which makes them useful for viewing popular topics.

Telecommunities (AKA Video Villages)
Groups of people who surf and comment on the Web while simultaneously watching television.

Thumbnail
A small image that represents a larger one. Typically is clickable to another page, image or photo album.

Trackback
A trackback allows Web authors to see who is referencing their material. A computer essentially sends a request from Site A to Site B, known as a "ping." When Site B receives the ping, it automatically goes back to Site A to check for the particular link. If the link exists, it's recorded.

Trigger
An event that gets a prospect thinking about about making a purchase.

Tweet
A Twitter message or post.

Unique Selling Proposition (USP)
A marketing concept referring to a combination of attributes, such as the chosen niche, competencies, products and services, that set a business apart from other ones.

Upload
Transferring a file to a computer.

Upstream (see downstream)
Websites visited before the current site the visitor is on.

URL (Universal Resource Locator)
The address of a Web page.

Value Proposition
The benefit a business claims they will bring to people in their target market.

Velocity
Speed at which information spreads from one website to another, its direction, and if it's rising or falling, can indicate how relevant, useful, popular or viral it is.

Viral Growth
Measures the number of people who share some bit of information or a story, where it's being shared and who's getting it. Indicates how relevant or important it is to these people and their networks.

Vlog
A blog that primarily features videos.

Web 2.0
Database-driven web applications, or websites that let you do stuff or more than just a brochure-ware website.

Website Builder
A tool used for creating websites, which comes in two forms. One is desktop software created specifically for that purpose, such as Adobe Dreamweaver. The other is provided online by Web hosting companies, such as Squarespace, which are typically designed for less technical users.

Widget (AKA module, snippet or plug-ins)
A small software tool that may be embedded in a website or added to person's social profile to provide specific functionality.

XML (Extensible Markup Language)
A standard set of coding rules for the Internet. XML was designed to transport, store and describe information, as opposed to HTML, which focuses on how information is displayed. XML-based languages include: RSS, Atom, SOAP and XHTML.

INDEX

A

action, 97
activity wall, user stream, 34
AddThis, 47
ad hoc, 161
advertising, 76
affinity groups, 32
aggregate, 74
AIDA Concept, 97
algorithm, 18
allocation, 53, 87
alternative formats, 73
analysis, 178
analytics, 167
applications, 3, 6, 40
archives, 148
assets, 5
attention, 97
authority, 93
awareness, 15

B

B2B, 85
Bacon Salt, 80
behavioral targeting, 152
behaviors, 60
beliefs, 61
bizographics, 28
blog not required, 129
bookmarking, 5
bots, 12
bounce rate, 171
brand building, 16
brand loyalty, 86

brand promise, 16
branding, 16
browsers, 39, 116
Brusha, Patricia, 22
burnout, 206
business benefits, 12
business cycles, 160
business plan, 12, 53-55, 137
business users, 22
buy flow, 170
buzz, 44, 91, 94-95

C

Cadbury-Schweppes, 81
call to action, 101
candor, 187
capabilities, 106, 114
case studies, 106, 114, 211
chiclets, 46
Collectors, 26
Combs, Valerie, 153
competition, 7, 57, 82, 160
comScore, 153
Connectors, 45
consumer behavior, 28
content, 5, 21
contrition, 188
coupon code redemption, 166
coupons, 56, 75-76
creative, 156
creative risks, 111
Creators, 26
critic, 201
Critics, 26
cross-pollinate, 49, 196

ABOUT THE TYPE

This book is set in Garamond and Gill Sans. Claude Garamond (c. 1480 – 1561) first came to prominence in the 1540s when King Francois I of France commissioned him to create a Greek typeface. Garamond is considered among the most legible and readable serif fonts for print.

Gill Sans is a humanist sans serif typeface designed by Eric Gill, a well-established sculptor, graphic artist and type designer. It originally appeared in 1926 where Gill painted the fascia over a bookshop window. The font became popular in 1929 when it was used on promotional material for the London and North Eastern Railway.

ABOUT THE AUTHOR

Robbin Block, marketing strategist and corporate renegade, ha been evangelizing the benefits of marketing strategy for over 2! years.

Part geek, part creative, she combines the best of traditional and new media like nobody's business. She's given hundreds of engagin; and often humorous presentations that deliver a dash of economi theory with a healthy dose of New York skepticism.

She spends the rest of her time writing and editing for radic hoping one day to have a show of her own.

ENDNOTES

[1] 'Despite the fact that 77 percent of business technology decision-makers engage with social media on the job, most B2B marketers are not effectively using social technologies to influence the purchasing decisions of their customers, according to Forrester Research, Inc.' "B2B Marketers Need To Keep Up With Business Technology Buyers On Social Media," Forrester, 2/23/09, forrester.com (accessed 11/10/09).

[2] Heather Dougherty and Marc Fanelli, "Hitwise US Social Networking Report," Hitwise/Experian, March 2008, 7.

[3] "The Impact of Social Media on Purchasing Behavior," DEI Worldwide, 2008, deiworldwide.com (accessed November 10, 2009).

[4] Jon Gibs, "Social Media: The Next Great Gateway for Content Discovery?," NielsonWire, October 5, 2009.

[5] "Brand Impact Social Networking" study, Workplace Media, May 2009, workplacemedia.com.

[6] Mintel Consumer Survey

[7] Marshal McLuhan, Understanding Media: The Extensions of Man (New York: McGraw-Hill, 1964).

[8] Workplace Media, Brand Impact study.

[9] Sarah Mahoney, "Magazine Ads, Articles Play Big Role in Online Searches," Media Post's Marketing Daily, March 26, 2007.

[10] "Cone Business in Social Media Study," from an online survey conducted among 1,092 adults comprised of 525 men and 567 women18 years of age and older (margin of error +/- 3%.), Opinion Research Corporation, 2008.

[11] Cate Riegner, "Social Networkers U.S.," Netpop Research, January 2009.

[12] Sharon Jayson, "Older adults among newer members on social networking sites," USA Today, January 14, 2009.

[13] Martha Lagace, "The Technology Revolution and its Implications for the Future," Harvard Business Review's Working Knowledge, November 10, 2008.

[14] Charlene Li and Josh Bernoff, Groundswell: Winning in a World Transformed by Social Technologies (Forrester Research, 2008).

[15] Hitwise Report, 7.

[16] Amanda Lenhart, ""The Democratization of Online Social Networks: A look at the change in demographics of social network users over time," PEW Internet & American Life Project, 2009.

[17] "SocNets Have Tiny Effect on Brand Perception," Workplace Media "Brand Impact Social Networking" study, June 2009, workplace-media-social-networking-impact-brand-perception-june-2009.jpg.

[18] Patricia Brusha, "Social Media Demographics Defined - Marketing to the Users Generating the Content," hospitality.net, October 22, 07. hospitalitynet.org/news/4033428.search?query=new+media+marketing (accessed November 14, 2009).

19 "Age Groups and Social Media Habits," Media Badger, March 12th, 2009, mediabadger.com/2009/03/age-groups-and-social-media-habits (accessed November 14, 2009).

[20] Ibid

[21] Ibid

[22] Brusha, Social Media Demographics Defined.

[23] Media Badger, Age Groups and Social Media Habits.

[24] Beth Snyder Bulik, "Technology No Longer Just Kid Stuff," AdAge, February 2, 2009, adage.com/digital/article?article_id=134205 (accessed November 14, 2009).

[25] Ibid

[26] Emily Steel, "Marketers Take Search Ads Beyond Search Engines; Facebook, MySpace, iPhone Figure in Efforts by Pizza Hut, Others to Boost Online Exposure While Controlling Costs," Wall Street Journal, January 20, 2009.

[27] "The Impact of Social Media on Purchasing Behavior," DEI Worldwide, 2008, deiworldwide.com.

[28] For a quick look at social media consumption and participation differences in broad demographic groups, look at the great profile tool that "Groundswell" authors Charlene Li and Josh Bernoff have made available at: forrester.com/Groundswell/profile_tool.html.

[29] Brusha, Social Media Demographics Defined.

[30] Ben Pitman, "B2B Marketers Need To Keep Up With Business Technology Buyers On Social Media," Forrester Research, February 24, 2009.

[31] Laura Ramos and G. Oliver Young, "The Social Technographics® Of Business Buyers," Forrester Research, February 20, 2009.

[32] Ibid.

[33] "90% Of CEOs Request A Private Business Network That's Just For Them," PRWeb, February 14, 2009.

[34] "The Collaborative Internet: Usage Trends, End User Attitudes and IT Impact," New Diligence, October 2008.

[35] "State of the Blogosphere," Technorati, technorati.com/blogging/article/state-of-the-blogosphere-introduction (accessed November 14, 2009).

[36] "Harnessing the Power of Blogs," BuzzLogic and JupiterResearch, August 2008, marketingcharts.com/online/blogs-influence-consumer-purchases-more-than-social-networks-6616/jupiter-buzzlogic-blog-readers-trust-content-purc hase-decisions-october-2008jpg (accessed November 14, 2009).

[37]160 characters is the norm for mobile phones, but the remaining 20-character difference between the 140 characters allowed for Twitter and the 160 is probably used for what is known as overhead – what the system uses for message identification.

[38] 'MarketingCharts, the survey, which echoes prior research from Rubicon, found that 34% of American consumers bought a product or service based on a recommendation from a friend or relative, while 25% bought based upon a recommendation from their spouse or partner; only 5% bought a product based on a referral based on what a blogger had to say about it.' Mintel Consumer Survey, 2009, marketingcharts.com/topics/behavioral-marketing/real-life-recommendations-beat-online-by-wide-margin-9345/mintel-recommendation-sour ces-in-person-online-product-service-june-2009jpg (accessed November 14, 2009).

[39] Ibid.

[40] "Fair comment," Economist, March 7-13th, 2009, 14-16.

[41] Heather Dougherty and Marc Finelli, "US Social Networking Report, Driving Opportunities Through Participatory Marketing," Hitwise and Experian Marketing Services, March 2008.

[42] Mike Phillips, "RSS: Consumers Don't Care and Marketers Shouldn't Bother," Website Magazine, December 15, 2008, websitemagazine.com/content/blogs/website_magazine_consumer_corner/archiv e/2008/12/15/website-magazine-s-great-rss-debate-and-challenge.aspx (accessed November 14, 2009).

[43] Hitwise Report, 6.

[44] Duncan Houldsworth, "Why Geography Matters in Marketing Strategy - The Spatial Dimension to Customer Communications and Marketing," Applied Geographic Solutions, 6/10/03.

[45] Lisa E. Phillips, "Affluents Online: Living the Luxe Life in Private," eMarketer, May 2009. Also, "MyLuxury: Affluent Use Social Sites Too," ModernJeweler, November 16, 2007.

[46] Jairo Senise,"Who Is Your Next Customer?," Strategy+Business, August 29, 2007, strategy-business.com/article/07313 (accessed November 15, 2009).

[47] Anthony Acquisti, "Online: Small Social Networks Get Big Marketing Influx," Brandweek, 4/28/08, brandweek.com/bw/esearch/article_display.jsp?vnu_content_id=1003794930 (accessed 11/15/09).

[48] Lars Perner, Ph.D., University of Southern California, consumerpsychologist.com (accessed 11/15/09).

[49] John Gaffney, "Social Media Survey Fills In The Blanks On CFO Gatekeepers," DemandGen Report, May 12, 2009.

[50] Hitwise Report, 8.

[51] Shannon Paul, "Making the case for social media in PR," Shannon Paul's Very Official Blog, September 1, 2008, veryofficialblog.com/2008/09/01/making-the-case-for-social-media-in-pr (accessed November 15, 2009).

[52] Kara Trivunovic and Kristin Hersant, StrongMail Systems, June 15, 2009, strongmail.com/resources/blogs/email_marketing_insights/2009/06/social-media-is-emerging-as-a.php (accessed November 15, 2009).

[53] Hitwise Report, 8.

[54] Gregory T. Huang, "Mayonnaise Wrestling, Flavor Fanaticism, and Social Media on Steroids: The Bacon Salt Story," Xconomy, 11/20/08, xconomy.com/seattle/2008/11/20/mayonnaise-wrestling-flavor-fanaticism-and-social-media-on-steroids-the-bacon-salt-story (accessed 11/15/09).

[55] Geoffrey A. Moore, Crossing the Chasm, revised edition (New York: HarperCollins Publishers,1999).

[56] William J. McEwen, "Getting Emotional About Brands," The Gallup Organization, September 9, 2004, 2.

[57] H. Kelman, Compliance, identification, and internalization: Three processes of attitude change. Journal of Conflict Resolution, 1958, 1, 51-60.

[58] John A. Byrne and Stephen Baker,"What's a friend worth?, Businessweek, June 1, 2009, 32-36.

[59] Tania Yuki, "Keeping Score with Social Media Marketing and Measurement: Three Things to Consider Before Getting Started," comScore's Brand Metrix, comscore.com, May 28, 2009.

[60] Fair comment, Economist.

[61] A search engine will only list pages it knows about, so make sure it's aware of all your website pages. For Google, follow the guidelines found in Webmaster Tools.

[62] Dave Thomas, "Media Is On Demand - But Content Is Still King, The Three Screen Trifecta: Mobile, Television & Internet, The Nielsen Company, Q4 2008 Report, en-us.nielsen.com/main/insights/consumer_insight/april_2009/media_is_on_demand (accessed November 15, 2009).

[63] Michael Hirschorn, "The Web 2.0 Bubble," Atlantic, April 2007.

[64] Hitwise Report, 2.

[65] "How to Get More Twitter Followers: Some Methods That Work," doshdosh.com/how-to-get-more-twitter-followers (accessed November 15, 2009).

[66] Ibid.

[67] Maisy Samuelson, "Now Companies too have profiles on LinkedIn!," LinkedIn Blog, March 20, 2008, blog.linkedin.com/2008/03/20/company-profile/ LinkedIn blog reference (accessed November 15, 2009).

[68] Mintel Consumer Survey

[69] Steel, Marketers Take Search Ads Beyond

[70] Jeremy Liew, "Performance advertising success stories in social media," Lightspeed Venture Partners, April 24, 2009, lsvp.wordpress.com/2009/04/24/ performance-advertising-success-stories-in-social-media (access November 15, 2009).

[71] Stephen Baker, "What's a Friend Worth?," Businessweek, June 1, 2009, 34.

[72] Ibid.

[73] "The Effectiveness of Social Media Advertising," Inspire Media, inspiremediablog.com/?p=221 (accessed November 15, 2009).

[74] Greg Jarboe, "Blog Content Influences Consumer Buying Behavior," ClickZ, November 14, 2008), blog.searchenginewatch.com/081114-124722 (accessed November 15, 2009).

[75] Enid Burns, "Harnessing the Power of Blogs," BuzzLogic and JupiterResearch (accessed on ClickZ October 28, 2008).

[76] Wailin Wong, "Marketers go 2-way with social networking," Chicago Tribune, February 3, 2009.

[77] BusinessWeek, 2/18/08

[78] Prospectiv.

[79] Debra Aho Williamson, "Social Networking Ad Spending Update," eMarketer, 5/13/08.

[80] Sarah Mahoney, "Articles Play Big Role in Online Searches," Media Post's Marketing Daily, March 26, 2007.

[81] Nathania Johnson, "Consumers Ok with Social Ads, But Rarely Find Them Targeted," Search Engine Watch, 5/14/08.

[82] Hitwise Report, 3.

[83] Paul Bruemmer, "Are Corporate Web Sites Optimized for SEO?", Search Engine Guide, 8/05.

[84] Fair comment, Economist.

[85] Dr. Jim Macnamara MA, PhD, FPRIA, FAMI, CPM, FAMEC, "Measuring Up," Vol. 7, No. 11, January 2009, themeasurementstandard.com.

[86] James E. Lukaszewski, "Seven Dimensions of Crisis Communication Management: A Strategic Analysis and Planning Model," Ragan's Communications Journal January/February 1999.

[87] For a good example, search for the Shift Communications social media release template.

[88] You may want to seek legal advice if you're using material that's not your own and you're concerned about copyrights.

[89] Hitwise Report, 6.

[90] Thomas, Media Is On Demand

[91] Mark Hachman, "More Time Spent Social Networking Than on Email," PC World, March 10, 2009.

[92] Thomas, Media is On Demand

[93] A2/M2 Three Screen Report, Volume 5, 2nd Quarter 2009, The Nielson Company, 5.

[94] Thomas, Media Is On Demand

[95] Ibid.

[96] Ibid.

[97] "Mobile Internet Becoming A Daily Activity For Many," comScore, March 16, 2009.

[98] "U.S. Mobile Phone Subscribers And Internet Users," Silicon Alley Insider, October 27, 2009, businessinsider.com/us-mobile-phone-subscribers-and-internet-users-2009-10 (accessed November 15, 2009).

[99] Media Badger, Age Groups and Social Media Habits.

[100] Mickey Alam Khan, "Mobile usage gap is closing: Experian," Mobile Marketer, July 18, 2008, mobilemarketer.com/cms/news/research/1353.html (accessed November 15, 2009).

[101] Anita Hamilton, "Suffering From Facebook Fatigue?," Time, 4/16/08.

[102] Hitwise Report, 10.

Breinigsville, PA USA
03 March 2010
233526BV00001B/3/P